HAVE I GOT A DATE FOR YOU!

That hot new attorney in the firm turned out to be hot, alright—for your *brother.* Then there was the gorgeous blond who seemed like a great catch—until her husband caught *you* in the act. As anyone who's still searching for their soon-to-be-ex-spouse can tell you, there's nothing funny about dates from hell—unless they happen to someone else. This sidesplitting true-life collection of worst date scenarios will make you shiver, cringe, and gnash your teeth, but most of all you'll laugh . . . because none of these dating disasters happened to you!

DATES FROM HELL

KATHERINE ANN SAMON is a staff writer for *Mademoiselle* whose article, "Dates from Hell," brought an avalanche of mail from lovelorn, date-worn readers. She lives and works in the dangerous date capital of the world—New York, New York.

DATES FROM HELL

KATHERINE ANN SAMON

A PLUME BOOK

PLUME
Published by the Penguin Group
Penguin Books USA Inc., 375 Hudson Street,
New York, New York 10014, U.S.A.
Penguin Books Ltd, 27 Wrights Lane,
London W8 5TZ, England
Penguin Books Australia Ltd, Ringwood,
Victoria, Australia
Penguin Books Canada Ltd, 10 Alcorn Avenue,
Toronto, Ontario, Canada M4V 3B2
Penguin Books (N.Z.) Ltd, 182–190 Wairau Road,
Auckland 10, New Zealand

Penguin Books Ltd, Registered Offices:
Harmondsworth, Middlesex, England

First published by Plume, an imprint of New American Library,
a division of Penguin Books USA Inc.

First Printing, April, 1992
10 9 8 7 6 5 4 3 2 1

Library of Congress Cataloging-in-Publication Data

Samon, Katherine Ann.
Dates from hell / by Katherine Ann Samon.
p. cm.
ISBN 0-452-26778-1
1. Courtship—Humor. 2. Dating (Social customs)—Humor.
I. Title.
PN6231.C66S18 1992
818′.5402—dc20 91-34605
CIP

 REGISTERED TRADEMARK—MARCA REGISTRADA

Printed in the United States of America
Set in New Caledonia
Designed by Leonard Telesca

To Larry,
to all the people who told me their dating sagas,
and to everyone across the country
who gave me a hand along the way

Contents

Introduction: Lighting the Fuse

Try to top this Date from Hell:

Debbie and Steve had dated a year when Steve set the bottom line: They couldn't consider marriage until Debbie met his family. If she and his family didn't click, they couldn't get engaged. His family was Italian, lived in Chicago, and was very close and traditional. He planned to move back one day.

Debbie and Steve flew to Chicago, and she met the twenty relatives—aunts, uncles, cousins, and grandparents—who came over to Steve's parents' house for lunch every Sunday.

His family was wonderful, but Debbie was nervous. Still, she let herself be amused by Steve's great aunt, who talked to herself loudly, and by his mother, who prepared special meals for her tiny Yorkshire terrier, calling the dog "the best child I have."

Before lunch, Debbie poured herself a third glass of wine and roamed around the big two-story house. She heard Steve's father announce that everyone should come into the dining room, and she hurriedly searched for a bathroom. She considered asking for directions, but was worried that she might slur her words and ruin any chance of making a winning first impression.

She finally found a tiny powder room that only had a sink and mirror. Because it was an emergency, Debbie decided to improvise, using the sink as a toilet.

Debbie climbed aboard, and the sink tore out of the wall, pitching her across the narrow room. She banged her head against the wall and was out cold while water spewed from the plumbing.

Steve began searching for her, and eventually his family joined him. He called her name and knocked at the powder room. She didn't answer. He was about to move on when he saw water seeping under the door.

Steve and his father decided to bust open the door. All the relatives crowded into the door frame to see their future in-law sprawled on her back with her skirt up and her panties down, with a sink at her feet, and water gushing out of the wall.

Six months later, recovered from a concussion, Debbie couldn't believe that Steve wanted her to return to his family for another try at lunch. She didn't know what was worse: that she had demolished a powder room, that his family had seen her private parts, or that they knew she had been peeing in the sink. But Steve convinced her to put her pride aside and give it another go.

When Debbie arrived she was mortified, but midway through lunch she relaxed a little. Steve's family was putting the episode behind them, and so was she.

"See," her boyfriend whispered, "it's going great. They love you." He seemed so happy that he practically rubbed noses with her.

Toward the end of the meal, Steve's father, who had been away on business, arrived. Debbie winced when she remembered that he had helped Steve take her to the hospital.

The father was coming toward her. Debbie wanted to make a run for it, but this was her future father-in-law, and she had to give him a big greeting.

She took a deep breath and pushed back her chair. She could feel her heart beating and knew her adrenalin was soaring. Just as she stood up, stepped forward, and grasped his hand, Debbie heard a cracking noise and a little sound she had never heard before.

Still clasping her future father-in-law's hand, she looked down.

There was her right shoe. On one side of the shoe, she saw two large eyes and a pink tongue, and on the other side of her shoe, she watched a tiny tail gave one last thump. Her future mother-in-law's Yorkie must have been napping, curled around the leg of Debbie's chair, and when Debbie stood up, she stepped right onto its neck, snapping it.

She'd killed the dog.

When I first heard this "Yorkie" date, it was from Andrea, a friend in New York who is in the fashion business. Thinking this story was extreme, I asked Andrea if it actually happened. Andrea said it was the real thing. She had heard the story from her friend Marcy, who had heard the story from Ellen, who had heard it from a friend also named Andrea. This second Andrea, I was told, could put me in touch with "Debbie."

The second Andrea, a marketing coordinator at a New York brokerage firm, told me that her boyfriend John used to work with Debbie. I was only one step away from getting Debbie's phone number.

John, a banking attorney, said he didn't know the couple in the date. I'd have to call his former colleague, Jyl.

"Jyl is best friends with Debbie," he said.

Jyl took my call in stride. The problem was—you guessed it—she didn't know Debbie. Jyl said I should call her boyfriend's boss, Mark, a stock broker on Wall Street. Mark was either friends with "Steve," or he *was* Steve. Jackpot!

"Dead end," Mark said, "I heard this date over Christmas. I was sitting around with a bunch of guys watching TV and drinking beers and watching a Rangers game. Tell you what. I'm going to call my friend Jimbo for you. He'll know how to get you to this date. He's the Aesop of the gang."

Naturally, two possibilities had occurred to me. One, that this was a tightly knit group protecting their innocent friends Debbie and Steve who might not want to talk to me. Two, that the "Yorkie" date was made up.

I was telling all this to my friend Kathryn, a magazine editor, when she suddenly cut me off.

"I heard it a little differently," she said excitedly. "I heard his family was stuffy, kind of an old-money WASP family in Connecticut. The maid had shown the girl to the powder room. And the girl didn't know that the toilet was behind the second door, like it is in fancy bathrooms. That's why she climbed up on the sink. And the ending is different: I heard that she plopped on a sofa, and the dog was curled in the little needlepoint cushions. And she sat on the dog and broke its neck that way. It was a Shih-Tzû, by the way. The story's true."

Maybe the Yorkie story was true; enough people had heard it.

She gave me the number for Ron, a magazine advertising sales representative, who was supposed to be friends with Debbie.

Ron had heard this version at a dinner party. He told me to call Liz. Liz issued a correction: The wealthy family lived in New Jersey. "And you're in luck," Liz said that Friday afternoon. "I'm having lunch with my cousin in five minutes. Debbie's one of my cousin's girlfriends!"

Of course, Debbie turned out to be the *friend* of one of Liz's cousin's friends.

This date existed in a parallel universe, with two practically identical versions circulating simultaneously.

A lot of people would like to meet the real Debbie and Steve, if they exist. But even if this Yorkie date isn't true, it's taken on a life of its own.

This is the kind of adventure we chronicle and pass on. Instead of gathering around a campfire, swapping Wild West tales, we sit around a TV set, or at a dinner table or a bar, wincing while this urban myth unfolds.

A whopper like this knocks on our darkest dating fears. It has such a strong draw because everyone has been on a lousy date, and almost everyone has been on a Date from Hell. If you're lucky enough to have escaped, count your blessings. Because if you date long enough, your number is bound to come up.

From the "Match Game" to "Love Connection" to the board game "Mystery Date," dating is billed as an innocent, exciting, promising lark—that we hope will lead to love. Which is why we date, which is why we suffer through Dates from Hell, and which is why we love to take solace in hearing delicious, disastrous dating stories. We all know that dating can be perilous, and it helps to know we are not alone.

One man asked me, "Do thirty-seven no-shows equal one Date from Hell?" I suppose so. Any man who has suffered through that many evenings of being stood up, and is still dating, deserves recognition here.

In contrast to the stories included here, stories like "We reached for the same box of cereal at the same time, and got married a month later" are cute—but what are the odds of this occurring routinely? As a single friend whispered after hearing one of these romantic anecdotes, "Nauseating."

Hearing a Date from Hell, on the other hand, has a rousing effect. Dates from Hell are the legends, the valentines with a bent arrow.

A Date from Hell is a set-up, a fix-up, a mix-up. It's a bust, a bomb, a wipe-out. And it's more than that: It's a short stick of dynamite or a downhill slide into disaster. This is levels beyond your basic awful date. You can't wait to tell a friend how you survived it, and your friend can't wait to hear about it.

In the following pages, you'll travel on dozens of hellish trips through the Twilight Zone. You'll hear the screams. You'll feel the sweat bead on your forehead as catastrophes are recalled by the survivors who lived to tell their tales.

These stories come from all over the country, from men and women, in a range of ages, who wanted to confess and be heard. This book exists because of these kind, frank people, who were willing to share their intimate—sometimes sexual—exploits, as long as their names and certain identifying details were changed. Read a few and you'll find you can't blame them.

Read a few more and your own worst dates just may seem, on second thought, a lot less traumatic.

The following Dates from Hell *can* top the Yorkie date, because they're just as much of a roller coaster ride—*and* they're all true.

DATES FROM HELL

1

Is this someone's idea of a cosmic joke?

First Encounters of a Haywire Kind

Hold on! This date's like a roller coaster that's popped the track and gone out of control. Even the best laid plans can hit a snag, but you're having to endure one ridiculous calamity after another, and there's no end in sight. Sure, anyone can forgive a minor mishap or two, but this series of disasters is so relentless—it's time to call it quits.

Daniel and I worked at a research laboratory in New Jersey, and I was attracted to him, even though he was unbelievably shy. I invited him to dinner one night, and we had a nice time.

Early the next week he asked me out for Saturday night. He had bought *Phantom of the Opera* tickets—which usually take a year to get—from a friend. The itinerary sounded great: We'd drive into Manhattan, put the car in a garage, have a drink, see the show, then go to dinner. He was pulling out all the stops.

Halfway to the city the car broke down, and we coasted to the shoulder of the turnpike. Daniel lifted the hood and poked around, getting oil all over himself. It was 6:30.

We started walking, and I was getting mad, because he wasn't talking, just fuming, and I had trouble keeping up with him in my heels. A mile or so later we finally made it to a gas station.

It took forty-five minutes before the guy at the gas station got around to calling a tow truck for the car. Daniel said he'd pay anyone twenty dollars for a lift to a bus line to Manhattan. So we climbed into a rickety old pickup truck at 8:30. The show had started at 8:00.

We waited twenty minutes for the bus, got into the city, and grabbed a cab to the theater. It was 10 P.M. when we got there. I wanted to blow off the show, but Daniel hissed one of his first full sentences—that he'd paid a bundle for the tickets, and we were going to see it.

We saw some of it—the last thirty minutes. I was tired and wanted to go home, but Daniel had made reservations at a restaurant on the Upper East Side.

The bill came and Daniel went white when he saw it. Haltingly, he said, "I didn't bring enough money." Dinner had come to more than a hundred dollars. Luckily I had some cash, and between us we could cover the bill, with a little left over to get us home. But that meant we couldn't leave a tip. While Daniel sat silently, in shock, I guess, I asked the annoyed waiter for a business card, promising I would mail his tip to the restaurant.

Outside, Daniel kept repeating that he couldn't understand how the bill had come to so much. On the way to the subway, he told me about a date he'd had a year ago. He had taken a girl cross-country skiing but had accidentally chosen the advanced trail. He had fallen on her, and she had broken her arm. What a riot, right? That was the most he'd said to me all night.

Our subway car was fairly deserted, and Daniel was staring at everyone with this wide-eyed "mug me" look, so someone did. Daniel emptied all our bus money into the guy's hand and said, "Would you mind giving me back a quarter so I can make a call to get home? Please?" The guy gave it to him.

While we were on 42nd Street, walking to the bus station, Daniel was glowing about his skill at connecting with people. I asked him to help me figure out how to get home on twenty-five cents, but he ignored me, then he stopped walking. He had left his new suit jacket on the subway. But now it was about 1 A.M. He wanted to go back and look for it.

What were the odds of finding the same train, much less the jacket? When I said I thought it was hopeless, he shouted that I was selfish. I said that he was insane if he didn't know that the jacket was already on somebody's back, and I was going home.

I stormed off, then realized he had the only quarter. I went into a bar and begged the bartender to turn the twenty cents I found in the bottom of my bag into a quarter, then I called my sister and got her answering machine. I made three collect calls to friends before I got through to someone—Mom.

It would take two hours to come get me, but she said she and Dad would do it. As recompense, I let her set me up on a blind date with her bridge partner's son, Ernie. That's another story.

On Monday morning Daniel accusingly told me that it would cost eight hundred dollars to get his car fixed—as if it was my fault—and that he had ridden five subway trains looking for his jacket. What a genius.

We rarely spoke after that. He was promoted—over me—a month later.

—Anne, 26, research assistant, New Jersey

× × × × × × × × × × ×

I missed the sexual revolution in the seventies because I married young and divorced late. But in 1978, the summer after my divorce, I decided to pull myself together and get in on the seventies while I could.

I moved to Boston and took a share in a summer house on Cape Cod, with the intent of having friends to go to parties with. I fell in love with a psychotherapist, who also had a share in the house. I didn't think he regarded me as more than a pal.

But on a Monday, the day after we closed the house, he called me at work, convincing me to play hooky and spend the day with him. It was a busy day at work, but I faked stomach cramps—"food poisoning," I told my frazzled boss—and raced home, more excited than guilty. My date had said he'd pick me up at 11:00, that we'd have lunch, and then "we'd see what the day brings."

At noon I had stopped having sexual fantasies, at 1:00 I had ditched daydreams of rushing to his hospital bed after his near-fatal car wreck, and by 2:00 I simply wanted his head on a stick. I was being stood up.

I called his office and got his associate, who calmly said, "Yeah, you're being stood up. You don't have to be Freud to figure that out. He does that all the time. He hates women—can't even be reasonable toward them in group sessions."

I couldn't go back to work after the dramatic food-poisoning scene I had put on, so I roamed around my apartment, taking stock of my love life. Sure, my ex-husband was a rat. But this was worse. My first postdivorce crush turned out to be a screwed-up shrink. I could sure pick them.

At 3:00 the phone rang. It was another man, someone I had met at a party that summer. I blurted out what had happened, and he said, "What scum. Listen, let me make things right for you. Meet me at the corner outside my office building at four, and I'll pick you up and we'll have drinks, and then I'll take you to dinner."

I cheered up, tacked a note on my door ("Sorry. I forgot I had other plans."), and rushed to meet my ego-boost.

After forty-five minutes of waiting at the corner, I heard "Hello!" and felt a swell of relief. He'd made it! Instead, it was the vendor of the tomato cart who was also doing time on the corner. The vendor asked me if I'd watch his cart for five minutes while he grabbed a sandwich. "Looks like you'll be waiting awhile longer, anyway," he said.

I was standing behind the tomato cart when a woman asked how much the tomatoes were. "Take what you want, and pay what you think they're worth," I told her, wondering how I had come to this.

She told me that even a cart vendor should be more professional and take more of an interest in the tomato business, and shoved three tomatoes at me. I bagged them, took her money, and was about to tell her it wasn't my cart when a policeman appeared.

"Where's your vending license?" he asked.

The woman sneered at me and walked away, and I explained to the policeman that it wasn't my cart, and that the vendor should be back any minute. The policeman said he'd wait, and after fifteen minutes said, "Likely story, lady. The real vendor is coming right back, right? Let me see some I.D. I'm issuing you a summons."

I got hysterical, which is probably why a crowd gathered, and why the policeman said, "Look, lady, I don't want to have to take you in or anything, but you have to cooperate and calm down and quit getting loud."

He probably wouldn't have handcuffed me, but at that point I figured my whole life was a bust that day, so I sat down on the curb and started weeping. I'd been stood up, stood up again, then booked for a vending crime that I didn't commit. Dating was hell.

The policeman asked me to stand up, and an attractive man stepped out of the crowd and said, "Officer, it really isn't her cart." Smiling at me, he said he'd been sitting at the window of a coffee shop on the corner and had seen me waiting. He told the policeman exactly what he'd seen.

The policeman told me I could go, and I mumbled thanks to the coffee shop guy, who said, "You got stood up."

I nodded, and he added, "Let me make it up to you. I just have to run to the bank. How about if you wait here, and I'll be back in ten minutes, and I'll take you to dinner?"

He seemed nice, and I almost said yes but stopped myself. I said no and went home. The day didn't have to be a total loss.

—Cheryl, 41, sportswear designer, Boston

× × × × × × × × × ×

Men were practically three deep around her at the bar, and I elbowed the lot of them until I was beside her. I skipped the opening line and asked what she was drinking. The other guys backed off a little when she told me "Jack Black," and gave me a look that I like to think said, "You're the one." (A buddy who was with me says the look said, "Freebies? Line 'em up.")

Anyway, I thought I had hit the jackpot at this bar where everyone goes after work. Angela was a fantasy come true. Besides being very pretty, she was successful, a co-owner of one of the hottest restaurants in Los Angeles. We exchanged numbers, and I left it at that—no hitting on her to go home with me *that* night.

Two days later I called and asked her to dinner for Saturday night. I made reservations at a top French restaurant and bought a thirty-dollar bottle of wine—nothing but the best for a connoisseur of food and wine. I'd be over at 7:00, we'd have a few glasses so she'd know I hadn't bought junk, then, after

I'd made a snappy impression, we'd make our 8:30 dinner reservation.

When she answered the door, her hair was greasy, she was wearing cutoffs and a stained T-shirt, and the place looked as if she had just moved in. There were boxes everywhere.

I asked her how long she'd had the apartment, and she said, "Couple of weeks."

Then she said she was making cassettes of her records and plopped down on the floor near the stereo. I sat on the couch and made small talk while I kept glancing at my watch. At 7:30 I said, "Are you going to be ready to go in a few minutes?"

"Oh, that reminds me," she said, hopping up. "Could you do me a favor? I need some help moving my furniture around."

I moved an armoire, a couch, a chair, the coffee table and dining room table around, still smiling to make a good impression. I moved everything in twenty minutes. If Angela put a hat over that hair of hers and put on some shoes and a long coat, we could keep the reservation.

"I don't think I like it," she said, pacing around the room. "I know! Everything out there!" She pointed to her terrace.

"Don't you want anything in here?" I asked.

"No. I want to start from scratch. With the living room empty."

I didn't want to argue, so I pushed everything outside, and it started to rain. I was horrified—that I'd have to move it all back inside, but she said, "That's okay. I like rain on my furniture."

Bells should have gone off in my head, but I was relieved I didn't have to lug everything back in, and besides, I was tired and sweating like a pig.

"I need something to drink," I said.

She tossed me a corkscrew and said, "Help yourself to whatever you brought."

In terms of making a good impression, I could have saved the thirty bucks for the wine and just brought over a dolly, some moving pads, and a jug of Gatorade.

I killed half the bottle, sitting on the carpet, while she spent forty-five minutes getting ready. So long to our dinner reservations. It was 9:15 before she came out and happily announced, "Ready!" She looked great, so I decided I was a forgive-and-forget kind of guy. And now that my perspiration had evaporated from my skin and clothes, I felt renewed.

We went around the corner to an Italian restaurant, and we both ordered huge dinners. I wolfed mine down, and she pushed hers around on her plate. I sucked down three scotches, she sipped a mineral water. "I'm a slow eater," she said, nibbling a quarter inch off a strand of spaghetti.

An hour after I had finished, she was still working on that same strand of spaghetti. I moved on to dessert and a series of cognacs, and then it slipped out. She was a waitress at a restaurant, not a co-owner. She had lived in her apartment two years, not two weeks.

It was 11:30 before the waiter pried her plate—still heaped with food—off the table. We'd been there since 9:30 and had been served around 10:00. I left him the tip of his life.

I wanted to call it a night, but she wanted to go dancing.

At midnight we went to a club, and she immediately ran to the bathroom. After twenty-five minutes she came out and said, "Just wanted to freshen up."

I asked her to dance, and she said. "Do you feel like having something to eat?"

I asked her if she remembered being in an Italian restaurant an hour ago, and she said, "I'm hungry *now*."

I asked for a table, and she ordered a swordfish dinner. Just as it came, she excused herself and was in the bathroom for twenty minutes. When she returned, she took a few bites, then excused herself to "freshen up" again.

By the time she came back to the table so she could push the fish from the left side of her plate to the right, I had resigned myself to our obvious incompatibilities. This seemed to be going nowhere. At 3 A.M., thanks to another waiter who jimmied her untouched dinner away from her, we left. I couldn't wait to get her back to her apartment so I could go home.

On the way to her place she yelled, "Pull in there!"

It was an all-night grocery store. I went in with her, and she loaded up a cart with enough food for a family of twelve.

I helped her bring the groceries back to her place and was ready to make a break for it, but she put her arms around my neck, gave me a long kiss, and asked me to stay.

Of course I stayed. I sat on the floor and drank the rest of the wine I'd brought over, and she made more tapes. I was seeing double, so knew I'd better step on it if I was going to make any moves.

She had some moves of her own that I liked, and she said, "Why don't you stay over? Get in bed, and I'll join you in a minute."

Yes! I tore off my clothes and flopped onto the bed and waited. I waited and waited.

I must have fallen asleep, because the clock said 5:30 A.M. and I figured out where I was, but Angela wasn't in bed with me.

I went into the living room and was pulled up short. I never expected what waited for me.

A banquet fit for a king was laid out on the floor: caviar, salmon, sausage, fruit, cheese, cookies, pâté.

Angela must have been sitting cross-legged on the floor, because she was tipped over, with her face smashed directly onto a large, half-eaten pizza.

I barely found a pulse and lifted her head out of the pizza box. No more pretty Angela. She had circles of pepperoni stuck in her hair, and tomato sauce all over her face and up her nose.

"What happened?" I asked when she opened her eyes.

She shrugged, pulled a piece of pepperoni from her hair, then popped it into her mouth.

"I got hungry. Then I must have fallen asleep. Want anything to eat?"

"What's the matter with you?" I asked, agitated. "You could have suffocated on a pizza! That's weird!" I sat back, realization and compassion dawning. "You're bulimic, aren't you?" I asked.

She screwed her face up and said, "What? Are you nuts? What an insult. I just have a really bad drug problem."

—Benjamin, 34, car salesman, Los Angeles, California

× × × × × × × × × ×

Stepping into my apartment, he closes the door and slams it on his trench coat as he walks toward me. I cringe as I hear the fabric tear.

His name is Jack, so we have some very strained humor about Jack the Ripper, and I hand him a glass of red wine.

I met Jack at a friend's party, and we hit it off immediately. Aside from being vice-president of a bank, he tells me he is also on the board of directors of a small dance company here in Minneapolis, a legacy of having an ex-girlfriend in the company. As we leave for dinner, he attempts to hand me his wineglass and somehow bats it across the room, splattering my white couch and beige rug.

At least he's mortified and helps me drench the couch and rug in club soda. He offers to write me a check, which makes me think I could really get to like a guy who is this considerate, but I refuse and tell him not to worry about it. Besides, there is something endearing about a man this elegant who is a bit of a klutz.

Pulling into the parking lot of the restaurant, his foot slips off the brake pedal, and we lurch into the pole in front of our space, creating a perfect semicircle in his front fender.

"This never happens to me," he says, sweating profusely.

I manage to get him to laugh about it and find myself enjoying the role of comforter.

We're shown to a great table in the middle of the restaurant. Jack is calmer, and I'm falling in love until we're served our entrées. Jack lifts our personal water pitcher, misses my glass, and drowns my lamb chops. I must be reacting too loudly, because people at nearby tables glance over and smirk.

We share Jack's entrée.

After dessert, though it's the middle of winter, Jack decides he wants to see what the outdoor patio looks like. As he gets up, his silverware crashes to the floor, and thanks to a considerable dose of practice that evening, I lift his coffee in the nick of time.

I catch the eye of the people at the next table and feel myself turn red. I hope they think Jack and I are on a business dinner and that it's nothing romantic. I'll die if I think one of them has whispered to the other, "First date." I sit up straight and try to look blasé.

A huge gale of icy wind whips through the restaurant, and everyone's hair suddenly flies in the same direction, menus are blown back against people's faces. The blast persists, and the maître d' races across the floor. I don't have to watch his path. I know where he's going, and who is causing the freeze.

I take a pen and piece of paper out of my bag, acting businesslike and pretending to balance some numbers, when the woman at the next table leans toward me and says, "Honey, some things in a husband you just have to live with," and winks.

Jack returns, excited about the possibility of bringing me here for dinner on the patio in the summer, and is reaching into his pants pocket for his wallet, when I see his elbow take a swipe at his water glass. I retrieve the glass and Jack drops his wallet, his credit cards spilling into a heap on the floor. I take a quick glance to see people suppressing smiles, and to find the woman *and* her husband winking at me.

—Laura, 30, English professor, Minneapolis, Minnesota

× × × × × × × × × ×

Gretchen couldn't have been a better prospect.

I was in my third year at UCLA, and my girlfriend of three years had just broken up with me. I knew that rebound dates are risky, so, being practical, cautious, and logical—and ready to go out—I asked a female friend to recommend someone to me. Considering I wasn't completely recovered from my breakup, I didn't want to make a big dating mistake. I'd have any prospect checked out beforehand.

Gretchen's stats were ideal: brunette, dean's list, nice, and she wasn't a party girl. She was a studious but well-liked person, who had a good social life. My kind of girl.

A movie and pizza made us both happy, and afterward we went to my apartment to watch a video and have a few beers. It was Sunday night, and at 2 A.M., as I tidied up, she told me she'd decided to stay the night—but we were not to have sex.

I figured she didn't want me to have to take the bus with her back to her place, and then have to come back home, which was considerate of her. I offered her the couch, and I went to bed, thinking that I wouldn't mind seeing her again.

The next night our matchmaker called and said, "Hey, it didn't take you long at all! Gretchen told a friend of mine that you two are an item."

An item? I explained that her friend must have misunderstood Gretchen, that nothing happened.

That night, when I came home from the library, there was Gretchen, sitting in front of my apartment door. The super took me aside as I was about to go up the stairs to my landing and said, "She's been sitting there for three or four hours, waiting for you. What's the story?"

I asked Gretchen why she waited so long, and she just giggled. I asked her inside, and she just giggled some more and left.

As I was leaving a 9 A.M. class the next day, Tuesday, she sidled up to me, giggled, then darted off. At noon, I was standing with friends outside a burger joint, and she came up to me, giggled, then raced away. I was flattered and found it amusing that she obviously had a huge crush on me. My friends thought I was hot stuff.

But on Wednesday, she stopped racing off and began to stand beside me, never saying a word. If I introduced her to friends, she'd still just stare at me.

By Thursday I realized she was tracking me down and following me. I'd come out of the men's room, and there she'd be. When I was at a friend's party, she came out of nowhere and glued herself to me, occasionally giggling. I went to a basketball game with a buddy on Friday night, and she materialized with a girlfriend and took a seat beside me. The next Monday, I was in a professor's office, discussing a grade, when I looked up and there she was, giggling in his doorway. She got to know my friends on my apartment floor and would hang out in their apartments, waiting for me to come home so she could sit silently on my couch and stare at me and smile.

Our mutual friends said that Gretchen could talk and had friends—which made my complaints about her make me seem as if I were nuts. Rumors, generated by Gretchen, were flying that I was crazy about her but was too shy to admit it.

I'd wake up in the morning and look out my window, and there'd she be in the parking lot, sitting on a car hood, staring up at my apartment.

I was a star member of my rugby team, a confident guy, but in one week she'd managed to reduce me to the status of a junkie, hiding and shivering in my apartment, peeking through my blinds to see if she was around, begging friends to lie for me. I was a whipped dog, running scared.

I confronted her several times, asking her to leave me alone, but she always giggled and stared at me with these big hazel eyes, and continued to track me.

The final straw was when I was talking with my rugby coach during practice. I felt a hand snake around my waist, then shoot down the front of my pants. The coach had the same look on his face that I had—disbelief, but I also felt terrified. I wrenched the hand off without turning around. I already knew who it was. I was in my own collegiate *Fatal Attraction*. Soon I'd find rabbit stew on my stove every time I got home. What was next?

The coach said, "Is this the girl I hear you're engaged to?" and I heard Gretchen giggle.

—Steve, 24, advertising copywriter, California

× × × × × × × × × ×

"Of course you remember me!" he said on the phone. No, I didn't. He said his name was Franklin, and that we'd met the night before at a friend's office party. I had absolutely no recollection of him. He described me in detail from that party and said we'd talked, but I didn't remember him. I didn't drink alcohol, so it wasn't as if I'd had a blackout or something.

Franklin called every other day in May, and I kept refusing his offers to go out.

On the last day of the month, our anniversary, my boyfriend of four years dumped me, and my friends were trying to get me back on my feet. They kept telling me to go out with Franklin, because "What do you have to lose?"

Franklin wasn't a turnoff on the phone. In fact, I liked his sense of humor, and if he hadn't been so persistent, I might have caved in sooner. Instead, I said yes to his sixteenth offer for a date. He said he'd come by for me at 7 P.M.

I opened my door the night of our date and experienced my first silent scream.

He looked as if he had just stepped out of the role of a geek on a silly TV sitcom. What little hair he had was combed straight over his head, from the nape of his neck to his forehead. His suit was a large brown and orange plaid. But the worst thing about his outfit was the mass of gold accessories all over his body. I'd never seen so much jewelry on a man before. He had bracelets, necklaces, huge cuff links, three stickpins on his lapel, a collar stay, a tie clip, four or five rings, a bright belt buckle—all in chunky gold.

I was thinking, *How can I get out of this date?*

His first word, in person, to me was "Remember?"

When I didn't answer, he asked again, "Remember?"

Was he kidding? If I'd remembered, I would have hung up on him the first time he called.

I wondered what chariot awaited us, and there it was: a loud sports car, with bands of glittering gold metallic stripes wrapped around it. The seats were so low-slung that we were practically lying down once we got inside. It was like being in a Batmobile.

Franklin revved the engine and spun his back wheels, burning rubber as we took off.

"I'm very much in demand," he said. "You're lucky I liked you enough that I was the one calling you. Usually it's the other way around. Class people are always wanting me to take out their daughters, and sometimes I will, sometimes I won't, because my schedule is usually too full as it is."

I sat there—rather, I lay there, wondering if he were out of his mind. Maybe "class people" wanted him to be a bodyguard or chauffeur for their daughters, not to date them.

On and on he rambled. "Women look at me and they smell power and money. There's nothing I can do about it."

I asked where we were going, and he said, "To a new, very fancy place I think you'll like. I haven't been there yet, if you can believe that. I'm always one of the first to go to a swank restaurant in town when it opens. I'm known for that."

We had headed into a not-so-nice part of town—where I was sure the car had aroused the residents of the neighborhood: "Sucker's just coming into sight!" He zipped the car forward and said, "Here we are! Excited?"

It was a Howard Johnson's. Not that I don't like a HoJo, but after all that bragging, I had expected a four-star restaurant.

"Howard Johnson's?" I asked.

"How'd you know?" he asked, genuinely surprised.

"I can read," I said, pointing out my window to the letters spelling out the name at the entrance. "Do you think Howard Johnson's is a secret?"

His eyes got big, and he said, "You've been here before?"

He made a big show of tipping the valet by yanking a ten-dollar bill from a roll of money, then took me inside to the door of the restaurant and asked me to wait.

After a few minutes he came back and said, "I just tipped the maître d' fifteen dollars for a good table."

I didn't know why he'd bothered. We were so early that there were only three other groups that were seated.

We were seated in the middle of the restaurant, center stage, for all to witness and hear, while Franklin talked about himself incessantly, mostly about how successful he was and how popular with the ladies. I would sometimes nod or say, "Oh, how nice."

After dinner he said, "You're a great conversationalist. I don't want this night to end. Let's go somewhere for a nightcap."

I said I had to be home early, but he said he'd have me home by 10:00. It was only 8:30? It felt like 4 A.M.

All night, not one place he picked was what I had expected. For our nightcap, instead of going to a casual bar, he took me to the chicest nightspot in town. I didn't want to go in for two reasons. One, it was my ex-boyfriend's favorite bar. And two, it was where my ex-boyfriend had broken up with me.

I told Franklin I wanted to go somewhere else, because I hated that bar, and he waved me off, saying, "Nonsense. You're with me, so you're going to love it."

The bar was packed, so I decided I was in luck. Even if my ex were here, we'd never see each other.

Franklin told me he saw someone he knew and led the way to a group of people. I stood behind him and stopped listening to his conversation about the Batmobile's horsepower.

I was looking at the crowd, trying to see if my ex was there. The coast was clear. I didn't even see the group of friends he ran around with, which would also have been humiliating for me. I could imagine what they'd tell my former boyfriend if they saw me with Franklin. If I did run into anyone, I could save my reputation from being a complete wipe-out if I could keep them from talking to Franklin—rather, save them from having to listen to Franklin.

I relaxed a little. At least I was out of the apartment at night for the first time in months.

I heard Franklin say, "Yeah, I'm here with a date. Just another chick who can't keep her hands off me or my money, so I gave her some money and asked her to get herself a drink. Where'd she go?"

By now I was too numbed to Franklin's talk to be as upset as I might have been. All I could think was, *Give me a break.*

Franklin turned and said, "There you are!" Then he mumbled to me, "You'll have to introduce yourself. I didn't catch their names."

He wedged me into his circle. I put out my hand and was shaking hands with my ex.

—Ivy, 38, headhunter, Pennsylvania

× × × × × × × × × ×

My buddy Kev and I are sitting in his pickup truck, staring at the hordes of people streaming into a new country-western bar. We've been sitting in the parking lot for an hour. We're petrified. Neither of us dated in high school, and we graduated this afternoon, so we decided that tonight is the night we not only go hunting for babes, we actually talk to one. Every few minutes one of us says, "Well, should we go in?" and the other one says, "Na, we'll wait a little longer."

We go on inside, not because we're ready to mingle, but because we have saddle sores from sitting on his beat-up truck seat.

We grab two beers and hold up a wall. One of us says, "Should we ask someone to dance?" and the other one says, "Na, let's wait a little longer." If this is a typical night out for Kev and me, we'll have this conversation until midnight, then get back in his pickup, saying, "A bunch of dogs. Not one good-looking woman in the joint."

But tonight, all the way across the room, like a tiny moth on the horizon of a foggy morning, I see a blue eye winking at me. It belongs to a babe—she's no dog. She's sitting on a barstool, winking. Winking like there's no tomorrow. Squinting her eyes, puckering her lips. Winking like a Christmas tree.

I look behind me to see who she's winking at, and Kev smacks me on the shoulder and says, "Do you see that? That girl's flirting with you."

Over. I have a confirmation. She is winking—not just trying to move around a contact—and at me.

Kev isn't jealous, he's ecstatic. He says, "Go get her, and bring back one for me."

I say, "Shoot, tonight's my lucky night."

I am knocking people out of the way like they're bowling pins to get to her. I cut right across the dance floor, knocking past couples who are two-stepping, leaving them in the dust. I am racing to that woman. And the whole time she is winking up a storm.

I skid to a halt right in front of her, and her hair and a bunch of napkins on the bar blow back. I'm winded but say, "Wanna dance?"

She tilts her head to one side, smiles real big, licks her lips, and says, "No. Not right now." Then she smiles again.

My mouth flops open. *Not right now?* Kev has moved and is now holding up a wall nearby, and his mouth is hanging open, too. All that winking from her, all that racing from me, and "Not right now"?

She must have figured out that I am green green green and decided she would just play with me. I stand there in front of her and think, *That's a good lesson, Andy. If they're winking at you, let 'em go by.* I'm learning the hard way.

Rather than go back and stand beside Kev, empty-handed, I snare a little girl—I mean, literally. She's under five feet tall—and I keep my arm around her all night when we aren't dancing. The message is "Hey, everybody. She's mine. I got me one." I am like a dog with a bone: "I got her now." I'm not going to let her loose, or she might get away. I'm going to get me some tonight.

Kev keeps trying to hang around us, and I strong-arm him.

This girl constitutes my first date. So I buy her enough beers to float a canoe. When she says she's chilly, I can't get my jacket off fast enough to whip it around her shoulders.

When she says she's hungry, I hand her a bowl of pretzels I snatch from someone's table.

Around closing time I say, "Can I buy you breakfast?" I hope she won't mind sitting between me and Kev in the pickup truck. I'm grinning from ear to ear, and Kev, who has trailed us all the way around the joint all night, is in awe. Tonight one of us gets laid, and it isn't him.

She pries my arm from around her shoulder and says, "Get lost, squirt. I'm just killing time till my boyfriend gets off from work and comes to get me."

Lesson Two. Just because they're at a beer joint alone till 2 A.M., hanging on you and tapping your wallet, doesn't mean they're alone.

I tell this to Kev as we're heading across the parking lot, and he says, "Lesson Three is, Don't ditch your friend all night, or you won't have a lift home when you strike out."

Kev circles the block two times, passing me up and waving each time. Then he backs up and says I can get in if he can call me "squirt" for a week.

I couldn't care less. It's been a night of crash courses in women. Somebody should have warned me.

—Andy, 18, student, Oklahoma City, Oklahoma

× × × × × × × × × ×

I met a guy at a party, and a few days later he called. When he said we should get together, I invited him to a Vanilla Ice concert for that night, saying my date had gotten sick, and he could come along with me.

A friend in the music business had given me the two tickets—front row. How's that for impressing a date—two hot tickets to a great concert.

As soon as he said he liked Vanilla Ice and would go with me, I hung up and dialed my former roommate. I had some quick negotiating to do. I had originally asked her to go with me. I should have known that she'd be angry that I was disinviting her to a show she was dying to see, and even angrier that I was dumping her that night for a guy. Truth is, I hate it when my friends dump me for a date, and I suppose I've really made them know it, so I was in a hypocritical corner. As recompense, I told her I'd take her out for dinner anyplace she wanted. She had been quiet, then said, "Skip the dinner. How about this: I'll let you get away with it if I get to dump *you* at the last minute for a date."

I would have preferred buying her off with dinner, but at least now she wouldn't show up at my apartment, dressed for the concert, insisting on going. At least the night was going to be under control.

I checked my closet for a black suede dress I'd worn only once and couldn't find it. I tore my closet apart, then remembered that it might still be at the dry cleaner's. I jumped in my car and drove there, but they were locking their doors and wouldn't let me in.

"I just need one thing! I have a big date! Please! I'll pay you double!"

They shook their heads.

No sweat. I'd buy another outfit. I knew there wasn't anything in my closet I'd want to wear.

I checked my watch. Seven o'clock. I drove to my favorite boutique and told the clerk my situation. Usually I wanted to buy everything in the store, but that day I couldn't find one thing. I drove to another store, and there it was—a red dress with an off-the-shoulder cut. Except, the hem was torn and the zipper had broken away from the dress seam and was hanging loose. The clerk told me the tailor had left. The price tag read two hundred dollars.

"Pin me in if you have to," I told the clerk. "I'm buying it. Get a needle and thread, and help me. I'm in a jam."

By hand, I whipstitched the hem while the clerk did the zipper. The zipper still looked iffy, so I used safety pins on the inside of the dress to make sure the zipper wouldn't pull away from the seam again. It looked good.

I raced home and put the dress next to the shower to make the wrinkles fall out, and the phone rang. It was my date.

"I'm sorry about this," he said. "But my car broke down. Can you drive?"

That was all? A tiny little thing like that I could live with. I told him I'd be over in half an hour.

I reapplied my makeup, fixed my hair, and reached for my dress. It had fallen into the tub and was a wet, red, soaken heap. I could have screamed.

Jeans and a blouse would have to do. I ironed very carefully, certain that I was destined to scorch it.

At 8:30, I jumped in my car and took off, realizing I didn't know where my date lived. I made a U-turn, went home, and called him.

At 10 P.M., in front of his apartment, I honked, and he came running out.

"We have to go to a cash machine," he said. "I'm out of money, and I can't find my credit cards."

I checked my wallet, hoping I could cover us, but I was flat broke.

We drove to three cash machines before we found one that wasn't empty.

I was struggling to be good date material, and not be cranky and tense, but too many things were going wrong. My date seemed relatively calm, though. He kept flashing me smiles, and I relaxed a little. Turning my life upside down for him had been worth it. He was pleasant, cute, and we were going to hear my favorite singer. From that moment on, it would be a wonderful night.

By the time we parked, bought our drinks, and found our

seats, Vanilla Ice was already performing, and the usher had to kick people out of our seats.

We stayed on our feet, moving with the music, with a crowd that didn't want to sit down, either. I had never been in the front row before, and I was excited. I could tell from the one song we were hearing that Vanilla Ice was giving a hot performance. We clapped, and over the applause little beeps went off.

"I gotta go," my date shouted, pointing to the beeper on his belt. "I have a patient who I suspected would need me tonight. Let's do this again soon! You stay and enjoy it! I'll get a cab. Thanks again! That was a great song he sang!"

—Nell, 33, publicity department of
a cosmetics company, Brooklyn, New York

× × × × × × × × × × ×

I was happy and impressed when Gina nixed my idea of dinner or a movie and said she wanted an active date.

I suggested canoeing, and she said it sounded great, though she'd never done it before.

This was our first date, and it was the middle of May, on a warm, nice day. We drove to a river that a friend had told me about, and I put the canoe in the water.

Although Gina had never been canoeing before, she got the hang of it quickly. I was really into it and was startled when she said, "It's really awkward that we keep running out of conversation, isn't it?"

I hadn't noticed. I glanced at my watch and saw that we'd been in the water for two hours.

She said, "It's three o'clock, and I have to be home at six, remember?"

I had been hoping she'd forget. Gina had a date with someone else at 7:00 and had consented to going out with me during the day because if we didn't, between our two schedules, we wouldn't have been able to get together for a month.

I told her we could start back, and she confessed that her arms were killing her.

"Don't worry," I said, hoping that my knowledge of the river would make up for my lapses of conversation. "We're going against the current. Heading back, we'll be going with the current, and it'll be a lot easier. Piece of cake. Tell you what, you stretch out and rest, and I'll take over for a while."

The smile that Gina flashed me made me positive that she appreciated and liked me, even if she was heading home for another date. I was sure we'd go out again.

I started paddling back to our starting point, and in a few seconds realized that we had been going with the current on our way down, and would be going against the current on our way back.

Rather than tell Gina this news, I paddled harder and was trying to figure out what time we'd get back to my car, when the canoe flipped over, tossing us both out.

We surfaced underneath the canoe, banging our heads on it, and sputtering.

"The water's freezing!" She gasped.

"Forty, forty-five degrees," I said, then wanted to kick myself. "Let's right it. Grab this side, and push it over on three. One, two, three!"

We tilted the canoe halfway up, but so much water was inside that it was going down. Neither of us was wearing a life jacket.

A speedboat was moving past us, and Gina waved her arms and yelled, "Help me! I'm freezing!"

It was a boatload of guys, and they circled us, pulled close, and helped her aboard. I didn't know if I should leave the canoe and get in, too, but I didn't have to make that decision, because one of the guys asked Gina, "What about him?" and nodded at me.

She screwed up her face and said, "I don't care. I can't deal with it."

What happened to my outdoorsy date? Where had this prima donna come from?

The guy threw me a line and towed me and the canoe to the bank, then left. After they were out of shouting distance, I realized that they had dropped me off on the wrong side of the river.

I had to cut myself a little slack: Probably I hadn't been aware of being dropped on the wrong side with a submerged canoe, because while I was wrestling with the towline, Gina had been flirting with the guy who had appointed himself in charge of towing me. They'd exchanged phone numbers.

Gina had wanted an active date, and that's what she'd gotten. I wasn't sure what I had gotten.

—Walt, 33, landscape designer, New Hampshire

× × × × × × × × × × ×

If I had started crossing my eyes, I don't think Marshall would have noticed. On and on about himself. What a great job as a pilot he had. What a great living he made. What great places he flew to.

I pushed my food around my plate and realized that he hadn't even asked me the basics, like where I was from, if I had any sisters or brothers, if I could speak—given the opportunity.

I was impressed by one thing: Just as Marshall would pause, and I'd think I had a chance to mention myself, or to comment on what he'd just said about himself, he'd somehow manage to come up with fresh sagas about himself: an argument he'd had with a stewardess who didn't have enough respect for him, on one of his flights to Hawaii; a pilot who was jealous of his natural skills; a sexy passenger who'd given him a huge, wet kiss after safely navigating them out of a storm.

The night had begun on a sour note, anyway. Marshall had picked me up at my apartment, and while he was driving me to the restaurant, had made a sharp U-turn and said, "I can't believe you dressed for a burger joint when I'm taking you to a four-star restaurant. I guess we'll go back to my place so I can get underdressed, too." He'd told me to wait in the car, while he changed from his suit into slacks, a shirt, and blazer.

As he talked on and on, 9:00 crawled by—9:30 took an eternity. At 10:00, I figured that if we skipped coffee, it would be late enough that I wouldn't have a problem suggesting we call it a night. If only Marshall would stop telling stories where he's always the underappreciated god.

"You're bored!" Marshall suddenly shouted, slamming his fist on the table.

Heads whipped in our direction from other tables.

Yes, I was. But I had been that way for hours. I didn't know what to say.

My date smacked some cash on the table and loudly, furiously said, "No one's *ever* been bored with me. *No* dessert for you."

—Emma, 31, magazine editor, Chicago

2

Night of the living dud

Your Dream Date Becomes a Nightmare

If your date is a knockout, a success, a charmer, if things seem too good to be true—they probably are. What you see is not always what you get, because this is the mixed-up world of dating. Whether your companion is perfect in person or on paper, there's always the potential for a dream date to turn into a dud at best and a gruesome nightmare at worst. You can count on it: Just when the romance seems to be blossoming, that's when the bottom drops out.

The speedometer needle sails from 65 mph to 70, then 80, then 85, and his hands tighten on the wheel. Speeding through the night, I have no idea where we are, where we're going, or what will happen.

I had just moved to Phoenix the previous week, and a friend encouraged me to go on a blind date with Peter, a friend of a friend. She told me he was gorgeous, a genius, sensitive, amusing, and wealthy. Fat chance that such a package existed. But I figured, what the heck?

Peter is all of those things, it turns out, and more.

Tonight he picked me up in his new green Jaguar and took me to a great restaurant. He was easy and pleasant to be with, and I was completely enjoying myself. Until midway through dinner. That's when it started.

"You tilt your head just like my mother. . . . You hold your glass like my mother. . . . You and my mother are so much alike. . . . You look like my mother. . . . You laugh like my mother. . . . You have to meet my mother. . . . My mother would love you. . . . You'd love my mother." On and on this went, a phrase here about his mother, a phrase there about his mother. I was beginning to get annoyed.

We vent to a bar for drinks—"My mother loves cognac, too!"—and at 1 A.M. we had gotten in his car so he could take me home.

A few minutes later I asked, "I know I don't know my away around town, but aren't we going the wrong way to my apartment?"

"Yes," Peter had said. "I'm taking you to meet my mother."

I said, "Perhaps another time," and he replied, "No. The time is right."

So here we are, flying down an unlit road in the middle of nowhere, and the speedometer needle flutters at 90 mph. I have stopped talking.

I don't want to meet his mother. This is our first date, and it's a blind date. And it's almost 1:30 in the morning—certainly not the appropriate time to meet anybody's mother.

Peter is chatting along about how his mother and I are going to have so much to talk about, but I am not listening.

I'm tense, trying to decide whether I should open my conversation with his mother with an apology about the hour, or act nonchalant.

He coasts to a stop, gets out of the car, and opens my door. I consider refusing to get out, but he looks too determined.

I step out, and it's pitch-black. I can't see anything.

"The family country estate?" I ask, hearing the wobble in my voice as I try to joke about his wealth.

Peter nods, and we start walking up a long driveway.

"This won't take a moment," he says. "We won't stay long."

I can't see anything and am glad he is guiding me up a walk he knows like the back of his hand.

As we near the top of the hill, he stops, leans in front of me, and says, "Mother! There you are! Meet Patty! Patty, meet my mother!"

He's talking to a tombstone.

—Patty, 33, receptionist, Reno, Nevada

× × × × × × × × × × ×

We had just made love when it happened.

We'd been going out for three months, and I had decided that as soon as her divorce was final, I was going to ask her to marry me.

We were at her apartment, and she had gotten out of bed to get more wine. I was looking through her bureau for a pair of gym shorts I had left there. I opened a drawer, and there it was, on top of a framed wedding photograph. The postcard read, "Don't forget—I get in on Sunday. See you at the airport." It was from her soon-to-be-divorced husband, postmarked Thursday, only one day before.

I held onto the postcard and stared at the photo on the bureau, of her and me taken at a restaurant last week. Maybe I was misreading the postmark.

She came back with a bottle of wine, and I flapped the postcard and said, "I thought you were separated and in the middle of a divorce."

"Separated?" she asked, putting down the wine and trying to pry the picture out of my hand. She sounded genuinely chipper: "I am! He works in Italy a lot, and so we're separated for months at a time!"

I had one more question.

"Where do I fit in?"

"In here!" she said matter-of-factly, and opened a bottom drawer. I'd soon be taking my rightful place in a drawer with her other ex-boyfriends, all of us photographed at the same restaurant.

—Mark, 25, waiter, Washington, D.C.

× × × × × × × × × ×

Subways at 3:00 in the morning are never a good idea, but there I was, down to my last dollar and going home late from a party. I knew I shouldn't have been there. The train was practically deserted, so I looked down at people's shoes; you can't make eye contact or you'll stop being anonymous.

Two guys got on. One had really nice shoes—brown penny loafers. His friend was smashed. They sat next to me, and the penny loafers, which were closest, started chatting with me.

His name was Bill, and he was attractive. Sandy hair, brown eyes. Nice clothes. I had been prepared to have a hellish ride, but it turned out to be pleasant. He wasn't an ax murderer.

Unexpectedly he said, "I'm going out on a boat tomorrow. How would you like to join me for lunch? We could have a Saturday afternoon on the Hudson River." I said yes, thinking, *Am I a nut to say O.K. to a stranger on a New York City subway at 3 A.M.?* But it seemed like a classy idea. And I was up for an adventure.

The next day I sat at the appointed dock and waited. The weather was gorgeous. A yacht went by, and the people on it waved. I waved back. A sailboat went by and waved at me. I waved back. A tugboat went by and waved. And I waved back. No sign of Bill. A beautiful sailboat floated past and waved. I waved back. The tugboat people waved again, and I waved again. Then the tug started approaching. The crew was all men, and they were all waving, so I waved some more. It was turning out to be a nice way to pass the time.

And then who popped out of the captain's quarters but Bill. A tugboat?

He was wearing dirty jeans, a T-shirt, and a beat-up captain's hat, surrounded by a scruffy-looking crew. Where were the penny loafers? Where was the classy guy I had met? Oblivious to my reaction, Bill excitedly introduced me to his "mates."

Bill said, "I bet you've never steered a tug around Manhattan, have you?"

I said, "No, can't say that I have."

He let me drive, and it was fun. I had let my imagination run, expecting a sailboat, but told myself that a tug was cute. There was nothing cute about the way it smelled, though. I couldn't put my finger on it, but the odor was sometimes so vile that I was nauseated. The tug was beyond dirty and grimy.

At lunchtime the cook—who had a sort of leering expression—turned over a crate and pulled two smaller rickety ones up to it. That was our dining area. Bill and I took our seats, and the cook dropped two tin plates in front of us.

The food looked vaguely familiar. Two thin slabs of something. I took a bite. Over-fried bologna.

"How is it?" Bill asked anxiously.

I chewed the rubber, then shoved it to one side of my mouth, faking a swallow.

"Really good," I answered.

The unspeakable odor of the boat was getting to me, but

we were going upwind, so it wasn't overwhelming if I didn't take deep breaths very often. I knew that the ride back, when we'd be downwind, would be a lulu.

After lunch I asked where we were headed, and Bill said, "Staten Island. There's a barge we have to pick up."

"What kind of barge?" I asked, thinking that might improve the ride, add some excitement.

Bill looked at me as if I was an idiot and said, "Garbage. That's what I tow."

—Rebecca, 26, studio musician, New York City

× × × × × × × × × ×

Smooth, quick-witted, nice-looking—he had it all. And for a blind date, he was a 9. He was wonderful at dinner, and I sneaked away to call my friend who had arranged this date (my friend's friend worked with him) and tell her he was a winner. I hadn't dated in six months—had taken a break from the strange experiences I'd had through video dating and personals ads. This man made me grateful that I had waited.

We went to a noisy hot-spot afterward, and I thought I heard him say, "You're a f@$#ing beautiful bitch."

I choked on my drink and said, "What?"

"You're beautiful," he said.

I digested this, preened, and said, "Thank you."

"Can I get you another f*$%ing drink, asshole?"

"What?" I asked. "You're calling me an asshole?"

"Shove it, f$&# face."

"*What?*"

"Let's go to your son-of-a-bitch of a house for a f&^#ing drink, okay?"

"*What?*" I said, then got up and went to a pay phone at the back of the bar and called my girlfriend who had arranged this date.

"Oh," she said, then gulped and added, "I just found out tonight. There's one thing. I was going to tell you when you called before, but you said everything was going great. . . . When he gets nervous, he curses and can't stop. Is that a problem?"

—Elizabeth, 35, elementary school teacher, Cleveland, Ohio

× × × × × × × × × × ×

Turning her back on me was the only way she could handle it. Melinda had been like that for fifteen minutes, and it crossed my mind that she might have been awfully uncomfortable, because her chair was bolted to the floor. We were at a McDonald's, and her seat didn't swivel.

Last week I had called 411 to get the number for a movie theater, and being too lazy to pick up a phone book or scare up a newspaper had its benefits. I fell for her voice. Melinda had been my directory information operator.

I didn't know the exact name of the theater, and she patiently ran a few by me. Next thing I knew, we were chatting and laughing. I'm normally shy, and not a big phone talker, but I found myself at ease with her. Melinda had to go back to work, and I gave her my number and begged her to call me on her break.

We talked on the phone every night when we came home from work. We both loved water-skiing, hated foreign movies, loved the same TV shows and music. We both even came from big families. I hadn't talked to a girl who was this outgoing and lively or been this in sync with a woman in a long time.

I asked her out and held my breath. She accepted but said she wanted someplace neutral and public. I didn't blame her, which is why we were at McDonald's for dinner.

Talk about your extreme blind date. I had worried she'd be

hideous, but she was beautiful. Now I worried that she thought I was hideous, because after I said hello, she turned her head away. I never did find out what color her eyes were. Hazel or blue.

When Melinda wasn't turning her head off to the side, she was looking straight down while she ate the hamburger I bought her. She kept swinging her hair forward, and I kept wondering if it bothered her that her hair was touching the burger almost every time she took a bite.

The people at the next table were shooting us dirty looks whenever Melinda would park her head to the side. She was staring at the floor, but I guess the fact that she was facing them would bother anybody.

I put down my burger and said, "Hey, look. I guess you were expecting better. Don't worry about it. We can just finish eating, and I won't call you again."

Melinda mumbled something that I couldn't hear.

"What?" I asked. "Listen, are you just shy, or is it me? I'd kind of like to know, for the record, that's all. If it's me, I won't argue or make you see me again."

Melinda stared at the table and said, "It's me."

She said two more words, but I couldn't hear them.

"That's cool," I said. "Everyone's a little shy. But you sounded so confident on the phone. I don't get this."

Melinda took a deep breath and said, "I can't see you again, because I get too nervous when I'm with people I don't know."

"That's easy," I said. "We'll go out a few more times like this, and then you'll know me and you'll be talking to me. We'll be dating, and you won't even notice."

I thought I handled that pretty well. I wasn't going to let her get away.

Melinda shook her head and said, "No. This happens every time. We'll date over the phone. I've done that before. Okay?"

I said okay, but I never called her again, even though I wanted to. I didn't want to have two-hour phone conversations on Saturday nights, talking about what we were eating and what was on TV, or holding the receiver to a stereo speaker so we could play each other music. From then on I stopped being so chatty when I dialed 411. I didn't want to set myself up for another letdown with another pretty voice.

—Robert, 23, unemployed, San Antonio, Texas

× × × × × × × × × ×

"How many orgasms have I had?" she asks, teasing me.

"Three," I tell her again. "Two just now. One a half-hour ago."

Well, what can I say? I'm in my late twenties, and I like to think I've had some amazing sexual experiences, but I don't think I've ever been involved in anything this combustible, and I don't think she has, either.

We're in the same sketching class at night, and after two months of classes and flirting, Tuesday I asked her out, and now here we are at the end of that date, in her bedroom.

And she has just told me that she wants me to stay all weekend. Of course, I'll go home tomorrow morning so I don't seem too smitten, but I'll be back tomorrow night.

Tonight, over the course of two hours, I found her G spot twice, turned her on to a few acupressure points she didn't even know she had, and I think we added a new position to the sex manuals.

The phone rings, and she reaches for her nightstand to answer it, then says, "Hi!" There's a pause, then she says, "Oh, nothing," and glances right through me.

—Bryan, 28, sports writer, Portland, Oregon

× × × × × × × × × ×

If you hang out at a country-western dance hall long enough, you know who everyone is.

So in walks a guy, one night, who even puts Dwight Yoakam to shame he's so good-looking. Tall, well-built, nice cowboy hat. Naturally all the girls start buzzing about him.

He leans on the bar all night and doesn't ask anyone to dance. My girlfriends are saying that when the ladies' choice comes on, there's going to be a stampede of perfume running his way. I decide to take matters into my own hands and not wait for a ladies' choice.

I ask him to dance, and I know the whole place is watching me. In particular, I know that several women who are annoyed at me for flirting with their boyfriends are watching, and so are three or four other guys I have refused to dance with all night.

This new guy says, "Sure," and takes my hand. After this dance, the unwritten code of the place is that he's as good as mine. I've staked a claim.

When I lead him onto the dance floor, the deejay hits us with his spotlight—I guess the word has traveled—and I am ready to make all the women in the joint die with jealousy. He's good-looking, and I'm one of the best women dancers in the place. I'm ready for my few minutes of fame.

He slams me against him, and I feel the breath get knocked out of my lungs. He has my hand scrunched into a contorted death grip. A fast-paced Clint Black song starts up, which calls for a jitterbug-swing dance. Next thing I know, he's spinning me so hard I feel my neck snap. Then he twirls me right into a concrete pole that everybody else always dodges, and I wonder if my nose has been pushed through my head and is now attached to the top of my neck.

He is, quite simply, your classic bad dancer, your basic klutz.

He's taking steps that are three feet wide, so I'm frantically hopping to keep up and follow him. The song is almost over, and I wish the deejay would kill the spotlight, but my clumsy partner isn't through yet.

As the song comes to a big finish, he tosses me back, pulls me close, then lets go of one of my hands and tosses me back again, which might have been his one good move. Except he lets go of the hand that he is supposed to hang onto, and he flings me so hard I swerve off the dance floor and crash onto a table, sending beers flying.

I look up, and there's one of the women I know who would like to skin me alive.

"All the women in here are real glad that you're stuck with that spaz and we're not. And we all sure feel more secure now that there's not one guy in this joint who'd be seen with you, not even the ones you turned down all night. Here comes your cowboy now. Maybe ya'll dance another one for us."

That's when the deejay finally kills the spot.

—Dierdre, 27, singer, San Antonio, Texas

× × × × × × × × × × ×

She was dressed like a dream. I was used to meeting for drinks, during the week, with women who showed up in their just-got-off-work mess-with-me-and-you're-dead-meat outfits.

You know, those funeral suits with bow ties and orthopedic-looking shoes. Most of them actually loosened their ties and hitched up their belts when they sat down. One belted out, "Scotch on the rocks. Make it a double. I had a pisser of a day." Sometimes I felt as if I were taking out Lee Iacocca.

O.K., so I was a little fried around the edges. I was getting burned out on dating.

So I knew my dating life was taking a turn for the better when Sandra showed up. She was new to town, and my sister's friend met her at a horse show. I was told Sandra was a knockout, and knowing my sister and her friend, I knew that this blind date would be a knockout only in the bowwow category. But as usual, discriminating guy that I am, I said, "Give me her number."

You know the first part. Sandra was a babe. Blond hair—curly. Blue eyes. And she had on this kind of loose, flowy outfit, with a long scarf thing around her neck that would float behind her when she walked. And she had on perfume—it wasn't just scented deodorant. Every guy in the place watched her when she walked in.

Sandra was no empty-headed mental midget. She was fun to talk to. To tell you the truth, I guess it was fun for me because she was a good listener—I remember blabbing on and on, and how intent she was on our conversation.

We decided to go someplace else for dinner, and we took her car. At dinner things get a little hot. Nothing major, just two incidents of leg contact that I orchestrated and she didn't pull away from.

I asked Sandra if she minded driving me back to my car—that was my test to see whether she was interested—and she invited me to her house for a nightcap first.

We were at her place, in front of this huge fireplace that I made a fire in, lying on this great bearskin rug. (I'd never been on one before, and it was fun.) So the fire was going, and we were making out—not getting too far, but really cooking. So I was taking it slowly, which was frustrating, but after a while was a real turnon.

She said, "Let me get into something more comfortable," and I thought I'd died and gone to heaven. For one thing, the real action was about to begin. For another thing, no one had ever said that to me.

I loosened some of my clothes a little. I didn't want to take them all off or she'd probably freak out and think I was going to pounce on her. I went for the casual approach: unbuttoned all but one button on my shirt, unzipped my fly halfway, unbuttoned my cuffs, took off my shoes and socks. I looked casual, but I had turned these ordinary clothes into a quick-release getup.

I settled back and propped my head on my hand, figuring I looked pretty debonair and not at all threatening. She'd probably come back in some feminine thing I could see right through.

I closed my eyes and yawned, because it was late and I was kind of sleepy, and when I opened them, I was staring directly at two of the biggest cantaloupes I'd ever seen. I looked up, and there was this brute towering over me, with legs apart and hands on her hips. The cantaloupes were her calves. All she needed was one of those metal Viking caps with horns sticking out of it on the top and she'd be in business.

Arnold Schwarzenegger was looking down at me, and I was not in the fighting stance.

She had put on some crazy workout outfit that was made of black Lycra and had yellow and red lightning bolts running across it. Her neck circumference was bigger than mine, and her arms and thighs were gigantic, with muscles like oranges. She had on one of those tiny shirts that stop right after they start, and her chest and abdomen were more built up and muscular than mine. Where were her breasts?

Her gut was alive. It rippled every time she breathed, which was hard and frequent. I guess she was ready, too.

Then she started some odd mating dance. She stretched out her arms, then starting at one wrist, a ripple of muscle traveled across one arm, across her neck, and down the other arm. Then she reversed it. Next she did the same thing on both legs. This display of flexing and rippling muscle groups was not turning me on, it was freaking me out.

Sandra wasn't just a body builder. She was a body builder who had gotten out of control and was receiving training messages from Pluto. Her giant body was barely recognizable as a body. She was big. And strong, probably. Stronger than me. I hadn't worked out in two years.

Like an idiot, I watched two Dobermans leap over the back of a couch and race for me, charging for my face. Before I could get up, they were licking my face and straddling my arms and chest. I had gone past scared and was turning to stone.

I barely saw these two giant hands reach down from Mount Olympus. Sandra grabbed my waist and flipped me over the way you flip over a hamburger patty.

Those dogs were walking over my back, and I felt Sandra tug at the hem of my pants and whip off my pants in one yank, like the tablecloth trick. Except it felt more like taking the casing off a sausage.

I tried to roll over and sit up, but just as I pushed the dogs away, Sandra ripped my shirt open, popping the one button I had left fastened. She was reaching for the waistband of my underwear when I got to my feet and started running around the room.

The dogs were chasing me, barking, and this huge, lumbering giant was trying to block me from leaving. I scooped up my pants and shoes, and that was all I got, but at least my wallet was in there. I started running.

The dogs were chasing me as I ran through the kitchen. I saw a box of dog biscuits on the counter and knocked the box onto the floor. The dogs skidded to a stop, and I ran out the back door.

It was winter, and all I had on was my underwear, but I just stuck my feet in my shoes and kept going for a while before I put on my pants.

I was miles from my car, but I didn't care. Hitchhiking would be a breeze compared to what I'd just gone through.

After that, you never heard me complain about women wearing boring suits.

—Stephen, 39, tax analyst, Charlotte, North Carolina

× × × × × × × × × × ×

Playboy bunnies weren't typical of my dates. It was just my lucky night.

I have this routine I always run through. I go to the local singles bar, pick out the most beautiful woman in the place, and strike up a conversation, hoping it'll either lead to a quickie that night—at least I'm being honest—or a future date.

This woman was five feet eight, had long honey-blond hair, an ample bosom, and a tiny waist, and the tightest white dress I'd ever seen.

I told her she was under arrest for being so damn good-looking, and she said, "Let me see some I.D."

I produced my police I.D., and we spent the rest of the night dancing and flirting with each other. She had been photographed for Playboy several years ago, she said, and for a few months had been a Playboy bunny at the club in New York before it closed. She was a dream.

I could tell she wasn't going to go home with me. But I did ask for her number, and she gave it to me.

I called her exactly two days later—part of my standard routine so I don't look eager or uninterested. We made a Friday night date.

My plan was to go to this restaurant I go to every weekend. They make a big fuss over regulars, and this never fails to impress dates, even if it happens at the places they themselves go to all the time. Dates love to think that their date is important, and who doesn't like to be fawned over? Then we'd go to a chic, noisy bar where I'm a member; the exclusivity factor helps jack up dating points.

When she opened her door, I leaned close.

Was this the same person? Yeah, it was, but without being in a dark bar, and without the distraction of the blasting music and loud conversations, she looked noticeably older. The frumpy dress didn't help, either. A little bit of tummy pushed out under her belt—not much, granted, but I remember an absolutely perfect body.

She didn't ask me in, just grabbed her purse.

At dinner she was almost bitter. So long to the vivacious, exuberant woman I remembered. She had bills to pay, an old boyfriend who kept dunning her for money, a relative who freeloaded a lot.

Her real world seemed far from perfect and was obviously taking a toll on her outlook tonight. As for her body, I remember that my ex-girlfriend had one of those contraptions that looked like underwear but was a modern-day girdle. That could explain the perfection the night we met. Tonight I was out with her genuine personality rather than her party personality.

After dinner I told her that I was tired and had to go home, and she said, "I can tell a brush-off when I hear one. What happened? Why aren't we even going for a drink at that place you told me about?"

I didn't want to say, "Because being with you depresses me," so I stuck to my so-tired-from-work story.

I drove her home and walked her to the door. She unlocked and opened it, then turned around and looked at me. I could tell she wanted a juicy kiss, but the most I would give her was a peck.

I was kissing her cheek, when over her shoulder I locked eyes with a tall blond walking through the living room. Now she was walking straight toward us and saying, "Phillip? *Mom*?"

My date gave me a "Whoops!" look, and the other woman said, "Mom? I could kill you. He called for me, and you took the call, didn't you?"

They were still arguing when I looked in the hall and saw a dated-looking picture of a woman in a bunny suit, and a more current picture of a woman in a bunny suit. They could have been twins. I couldn't fault her mother too much—she'd been a knockout in her day, and was still pretty. Couldn't blame her for trying.

I closed the door and walked to my car, and I don't think they even noticed. They were two riled-up bunnies.

—Phil, 39, policeman, North Dakota

× × × × × × × × × ×

He called me from the butcher shop.

We'd been dating six months, and when he arrived at my place tonight, he said he'd be in charge of preparing dinner.

He had gone out for lamb chops.

"I'm at the butcher shop," he said. "I'll make it quick. I was number twelve in line. I fell in love with a woman in front of me, number eleven. Don't ask me to explain it. It's one of those once-in-a-lifetime things. I hope you feel like this one day. I'm not coming back. Good luck with dinner."

—Fran, 42, lawyer, Phoenix, Arizona

× × × × × × × × × ×

I was single and in my twenties, and my cousin had promised me that my date would be a gentleman—that he was almost old-fashioned he was so correct. He was indeed a gentleman. Impeccably polite and dressed, well-versed, and chivalrous.

He took me to a very fine steakhouse, and we had tickets to a symphony afterward.

As the waiter cleared our table, my date leaned across the table, took my hand, and said, "I would like to make love to you."

I was taken aback but collected myself and declined.

He countered that I was a very sexy woman, and he needed me.

I explained that I certainly would not sleep with a blind date and had no intention of sleeping with anyone until I got married, and when that day came, I would be sleeping with only my husband.

He persisted, giving me his view of why it would be good and necessary for me to sleep with him.

I politely held my ground.

He paid the bill and said, "In that case, would you mind if we skip the symphony and I take you home? I'd like to call someone else so the evening won't be a total waste."

—Christine, 70, retired pediatrician, Milwaukee, Wisconsin

× × × × × × × × × ×

Meeting someone for Sunday brunch is a dangerous idea if you don't know what to expect, because you're stuck with him for hours afterward.

He's persistent. I've said I have work to do, family to call, a dog to bathe, and he won't let me leave.

"One more cup of coffee," he keeps saying, flagging the waiter for endless cups. "Don't be a stick-in-the-mud."

For the last twenty minutes his pushy line has been "Don't be compulsive. Have dessert."

Out of forty replies to the personals ad I ran, his was the

first one I called. He's a management consultant but looks as if he lives on the street. His clothes are rumpled and dirty, his hair is greasy and straggly. I wonder if he knows that soap exists. His horrible looks aside, there's a major creep component to him—bad vibes, kind of sour and hostile. I can sure pick 'em on paper, too.

It's 3:00 and we sat down for brunch at noon. Enough is enough.

I firmly tell him I have to go, and I give him money for my share.

We're outside, and I say good-by. He says we should get together again, and I say sure, that'd be great. Anything to put an ending to this date.

I still can't shake him. As I walk toward my apartment, he falls in step beside me. I can tell he's angry, anything but subtle. He says, "I see that I'm not up to your high standards of dating material. Would it have helped if I had shown you the keys to my Saab? How about a bank statement? Would you like that?"

We're passing a string of sidewalk cafés, and just as he finishes his snide comments, I hear my name.

There's my boss, and she's with her husband and two of our clients, eating outside at the café we're in front of. Talk about sinking through the cement. My boss and her husband are both from old New England families, and probably secretly desire to rewrite etiquette books.

I wave and try to move on. Tomorrow I'll tell her that I was doing volunteer work for my church, and that the guy she saw me with on Sunday is a charity case I decided to spend time with.

But my date grabs my elbow and stops me. I can't move on.

"Who are they?" he asks.

Like a fool, I tell him, and he takes me in his grubby arms

and bends me backward. I'm too flabbergasted to push him away. He opens his mouth, unfurls an eight-inch tongue, and shoves it down my throat.

Try living that one down at work.

—Brittany, 23, public relations, San Francisco

3

The amazing creep show

Truly Monstrous Dates

Too preposterous for words, too bizarre to be believed, too frightening to be funny—this isn't a date, it's torture! You knew better than to get your hopes up too high, you expected the worst, but no one ever could have prepared you for *this* level of horror and anxiety. This date rocks right off the Richter scale of scary.

Greg was a tall, light-haired version of Robert Palmer, and after a couple of dates and steamy fantasies on my part, I was actually spending the night with him at his house. When I woke up beside him the next morning, I tried to pull my legs apart, but they wouldn't budge. I started to panic, trying as hard as I could to separate them. The first thing that crossed my mind was that Greg was such a great lover he had paralyzed me. Then I thought that God had gotten me for sleeping with such a good-looking womanizer. The harder I tried, the more impossible it was to move my legs. Then I felt something soft but firm on my thighs, and it was moving up to my stomach. I froze.

Greg rolled over, and I said, "You've got to help me. My legs are swelling and I can't move them, and it feels like something is happening to my stomach."

He whipped back the covers and said, "Oh. That's Daisy, my boa constrictor. You must have been thrashing around. That really irritates her and makes her tighten her grip. That's her head on your stomach. Any minute she'll come up to kiss you."

I opened my mouth to let out a scream, but there was no sound—just silence. His *what*? It was moving past my belly-button now, and I was afraid I was going into shock.

Finally I whispered, "Move it. Please. Hurry."

Greg seemed puzzled, but he moved the head away, purring, "My little sweetheart." Then, to me, he said, "She does this in the winter," but I couldn't see his face, because I really was paralyzed—with fear. I couldn't move my head, close my mouth, or make my eyes stop opening so wide. "She gets cold," he continued, "and sometimes she gets in bed with me and wraps around my legs to keep warm. She must have liked you."

What was with the proud papa stories? Wasn't he going to unwrap her? How many miles of Daisy was there? All wrapped around *me*? I tried not to visualize it, because if I did I would have to be admitted to a psycho ward in my frozen position.

I guess he noticed that I was on the edge, because he said, "I'll keep her head away from you, okay? Nod if you can hear me. Or move your little finger."

That snapped me out of it. How could he be a wise guy at a time like this?

I asked him to unwrap her, and he said, "Can't. If I try anything now, she'll contract even more. Give her about fifteen minutes, and it'll be fine."

Fifteen minutes? It seemed the same as fifteen years. Then

I felt his mouth on my neck—I checked to make sure it was him and not Daisy—and I realized that Greg wanted to make love to me with his pal wrapped around my legs! There was flat-out no way we could do it—Daisy had made that physically impossible.

Greg seemed to come to the same conclusion, and with a moan, he got up and turned on the TV. We sat up in bed and shared a cigarette. If you didn't know better, you'd think we were just contentedly watching a sitcom on the tube. He periodically checked to see how Daisy was doing. I was becoming resigned to the situation, though I couldn't bring myself to look at Daisy.

After ten minutes had passed, I closed my eyes tight and Greg unwound his pet. I still kept them closed when he said, "Open your eyes and take a look. She's really a beauty."

Yeah, right. I jumped out of bed, and from the corner of my eye I saw a fat rope about six miles long draped between Greg's arms.

I grabbed my clothes, shook them out to be sure there weren't any "pets" wound up in them, then ran out of the house—away from anything that could be slithering on the floor or hanging from the ceiling, poised to drop on my head. I got dressed in his driveway, checked my car thoroughly, then drove home clutching the wheel and screaming, positive that if I looked down, Daisy would be wrapped around my ankles.

—Liz, 28, dentist, Kansas City, Kansas

× × × × × × × × × ×

I feel glorious, like I'm in the opening scene of a movie that I'd love to watch, that would immediately hold my attention.

I've never ridden in a vintage car before, and here I am,

flying down the road in a 1957 Chevy Bel Air convertible. Red, white walls, red interior, and the radio works, so Preston has it tuned to a Beach Boys song. This is a great first date.

I'm sitting beside a handsome guy, in a great car, driving through gorgeous country, on a spectacular day. The sun is out, the sky's pure blue, and there are just two or three puffs of clouds overhead.

He's got sunglasses on, I've got sunglasses on. His hair is blowing in the wind, my hair is blowing in the wind. If I had seen a couple like us, in a car like this, on a day like this, I would have stared and drooled.

I'm thinking, *This is it! This is what life's all about! It doesn't get any better!*

All of a sudden, the biggest black bird I have ever seen comes smashing against the windshield, flapping its wings and squawking.

I'm screaming, and Preston is swerving on the road, because he can't see.

The bird is making "thomp, thomp, thomp" sounds against the windshield as it flaps its wings, and its eyes and beak look humongous. Preston keeps swaying on the road, trying to tip it off the windshield.

I put my head in my lap, and Preston is yelling at me to do something, but I don't know what to do. I lift my head and yell, "*What?*"

The bird flips over the windshield and falls onto my lap, and I raise my hands over my head and start screaming because the bird is flapping its wings all over my face and chest. Every time Preston swerves, the bird and I sway from side to side, and it digs its claws into my blazer to hang on. I don't have anything to hang on to, and I don't want to touch this bird. I close my eyes and scream some more.

I feel the car tilt and lurch, then stop. Preston is out of the car, opening my door. There is one moment when the bird and I lock eyes, and we both let out bloodcurdling screams.

Preston gets in the back seat and uses his jacket to try to bat the bird off my lap and out of my door. After five swats he manages to scoot the bird onto the pavement. It wobbles a little, then flies away in a low zigzag.

I am still screaming as I notice that the front half of the car is in a ditch, and that a small crowd is gathering.

A man pats my arm and says, "Was he trying to hurt you? We were behind you, and that woman over there was coming from the other direction, and we saw the car going all over the road. What was he doing to you? Was he trying to shove you out of the car while he was driving? Were you two fighting?"

I've stopped screaming, but I can't talk.

I hear Preston frantically say, "I know there's no bird *now*, but there was. It hit our windshield and then flipped into the car. I got it out, and it flew off."

Preston says to me, "Mae, come on! Tell them there was a bird!"

I can't talk, so I just nod.

The crowd thins a little, and Preston says, "Listen, Mae. It was just a freak accident. You know that. Are you feeling better? Are you ready? I'll drive you home. No more birds are going to do that again."

At the mention of that word, I still feel the bird flapping against my face and chest, and regardless of whether my eyes are open or closed, I can still see that moment when the bird and I lock eyes, and I want to start screaming again.

I have something to say, and it's important, so I make myself form the words.

"Can you put the top up?" I ask, also planning to roll the windows up tight. There's no other way I'll be a sane passenger in this car.

Preston grits his teeth and looks nervous. He looks up the road and down the road, then back at me.

"Can't," he says, "it's broken."

—Mae, 29, chef, Ohio

× × × × × × × × × × ×

She is showing me around her house. She just had it built, and though it's small, it's really nice.

It's our first date—we met at a CPR class. I'm taking her out for dinner.

She's showing me every room, and I'm trying to pay attention, but it's difficult for me, because I'd rather look at her. She's pretty and petite.

The house isn't my taste—too frilly. Frilly curtains, frilly bedspreads, but it looks as if it could be in a home magazine, it's so completely and neatly decorated.

She leads me to the kitchen, and I decide I'm hallucinating.

There is a pig in her kitchen. Sitting in a huge metal tub—big enough for a human to bathe in—is a pig. A whole pig, three or four feet of pig, with ears and eyes and a tail, floating in water and staring a hole through me. When it dawns on me that it's dead, I don't feel much relieved.

"Oh. I love pork. I like to make my own," she says, sounding carefree. "I need to let this pig get cleaned out a little before I chop it up. I'm letting it soak. Can you imagine how many newspapers I'll have to put down on the floor and counter when I get going on chopping it up? It's going to get pretty messy in here! It's a big one, isn't it?"

She laughs, one of those delicate, ladylike laughs, and says, "Just think! If you marry me, you'll have fresh pig all the time!"

Marry her? I can't wait to ditch her. I'm a vegetarian.

—Rodney, 23, yoga instructor, Pittsburgh

× × × × × × × × × ×

My former college roommate, who had been the campus beauty, gave me strict instructions. "Dress up," she said, without adding, "for once in your life."

She had given my number to one of her co-workers, Guy. Guy would be calling me. She told me that Guy was from Paris, always dressed in designer clothes, had dark features, a great body, looked like a model. The only negative thing about him was that he was a bit of a priss about his outfits. "He never has a stain or a loose button or a wrinkle," my friend said. "So skip the blue jeans and wear a dress. Get it dry-cleaned."

He sounded great on the phone—it was the first time I'd be going out with someone who had a sexy French accent.

He wanted me to meet him at his apartment, and I didn't have a problem with that. I felt safe meeting there, considering his entire office knew we had a date.

His apartment building was very classy, and I was glad I'd gone to the trouble not just to dry-clean a dress, but to have a manicure.

The doorman rang the apartment and announced my arrival, then sent me up.

I rang the doorbell, and Guy answered. He was definitely good-looking. But he was dressed for staying home alone. He had on grubby jeans, was barefoot, and his hair was messed up.

"Come in," he said. "I'll just be a minute."

"Did you forget we were going to dinner?" I asked.

"No, no. I'm just late. Please, sit."

Forget it.

It was a studio apartment, and the floor was covered with pizza boxes, newspapers, paper bags. The sofa bed was pulled out, and it was stacked with clothes piled about two feet high. There was one chair, and it was piled with clothes, too.

I decided to stand.

Guy smiled and went into the bathroom, carrying some additional clothes.

Now that he was in a separate room, I let my guard down and made a face. The apartment smelled horrible.

I peeked in the kitchen and was completely grossed out. Dirty dishes and pots were stacked in the sink and on the counters. There were large pots on the floor, and one of them had something like old spaghetti sauce encrusted on the sides. Fruit flies were swarming around a garbage pail that had overflowed.

"All ready!" Guy called cheerfully.

I went back in the living room, and there he was, looking terrific. Maybe he could pull together a good outfit, but Mr. Neat-As-a-Pin was a consummate slob at home. No one would ever have known.

As long as we got out of the apartment, we had a good chance of having a nice time. I'd just have to tell myself that this was a dinner date, not a lifetime commitment to marry a pig.

"I just need a jacket," he said.

To my shock he reached to the bottom of one of the biggest piles on the sofa bed, yanking out a navy blazer. I waited for him to say he had to iron it or steam it. At the least, I thought he'd shake it out. Instead, he just put it on. It looked good. I don't know how he did it.

We were leaving his apartment, headed for a cozy French restaurant that he was telling me about.

"They only have little booths for two. We have to sit side by side, very close. Okay?" he asked as I stepped past him, heading into the hallway. I could feel his breath on my neck, and I thought, *Things are looking up. This guy is hot. Maybe I can overlook his slob side.*

That's when I saw the huge cockroach on his shoulder. It was about two inches long, with even longer antennae.

I jumped back and said, "Oh, my God! There's a cockroach on your shoulder!"

He smiled and said, "Does that bother you? If so, okay," and casually flicked it in my direction, which made me scream, because I hate cockroaches.

How could he live like that? With cockroaches turning his mounds of clothes into highways and hotels?

I told myself to chill out. That it could happen to anyone.

Then I saw a smaller one on his neck.

That time, I just pointed.

He put his hand to his neck, then brought his hand down. The cockroach was resting on the top of his hand. He waved his hand, and it fell off.

"Whose car should we take?" he asked, and I realized that I felt sick.

He was crawling with roaches. I didn't want him to infest my car. I didn't want to ride in his infested car. Nor did I think I could spend a cozy evening at a restaurant, sitting close to him, watching roaches crawl over him. And crawl onto me. My skin was already itching, and my stomach felt queasy. I was imagining roaches crawling up my legs. I hadn't had a roach in my apartment in years, mainly because I have the place exterminated religiously. I take no chances where roaches are concerned. I hate them. How could I go anywhere with this walking roach farm?

"Your car. No. My car," I said, deciding to brave this out. I could handle the situation, I convinced myself. We were walking to the elevator, and I saw the first roach, the gigantic one, slip back under Guy's apartment door. That was the turning point.

I grabbed my stomach and resorted to the old "Oh, no! I feel sick! I have to go home" gambit, unused since high school.

Every time Guy tried to touch me, to comfort me, I got semihysterical, putting him off politely while the whole time

I was thinking, *Get back! Get away from me! Don't touch me, you roach king.*

When the elevator arrived, I jumped on and pumped the "close" button, waving good-by.

A few days later I found a medium-size roach on my kitchen counter. It was just a coincidence, right? I hadn't carried it into my apartment on my body, right?

—Jennifer, 24, sculptor, Portland, Maine

× × × × × × × × × ×

She has taken over my life, and I can't get it back.

We met while we were on summer vacation in British Columbia. I was at the hotel restaurant, having breakfast, and the hostess pushed us together, saying that since we were both eating alone and the place was full, "You won't mind if this young woman joins you, will you?"

I didn't mind. Ruth was pretty. What I minded was when my traveling companion joined us. Lloyd invited her to go on the rest of the road trip with us, and she accepted.

She was staying at another hotel but didn't go back for any of her things. She had a small bag with her, since she had planned for a day trip, and said that was all she needed.

When she went to the counter for more coffee, I whispered to Lloyd that he was out of his mind, and he whispered back to me to loosen up and take some chances for once in my life.

If I thought Ruth was a flake that morning, that afternoon I thought she was exciting and easy to be with, and definitely added a sense of humor to the trip. She was focused more on me than on Lloyd, and I joked that if we imagined that Lloyd was our chauffeur, Ruth and I would be on a very unusual date. These days Lloyd reminds me of that crack regularly.

Ruth didn't expect a free ride. She paid for her own meals and chipped in on the hotel rooms. To save money, we'd book one room with two beds, and she slept with me, because she said Lloyd's snoring was horrible. It was, but Lloyd and I doubted that that was the reason. We slept in sweat clothes, and there was no hanky-panky.

At the end of the week, when we parted ways with her, I had to admit that I would miss her.

Back in California, I kept thinking about her and finally called her in Miami. After a month of phone calls, in October I flew out to see her, then she came to see me the next month. The second time I went to Miami, at the end of December, I asked her to move in with me.

I thought she'd want to think it over, but just as in British Columbia, she said sure.

This is as good a time as any to mention that she has four kids: two of her own from her marriage, and her two stepchildren—of whom she had informal custody—from her ex-husband's prior marriage. This didn't bother me. I like kids.

We'd have plenty of room. I had a huge, two-story house. Ruth had fallen in love with it when she'd come to visit me.

I called Lloyd, the same spontaneous guy who'd invited her along on our trip, to tell him the good news, and he sounded stupefied that I had invited her and her kids to move in with me.

I told him that having a best friend and new girlfriend who were both spontaneous had rubbed off on me. He sounded as if he was choking.

I took the following week off from work, arranged for someone to drive out her car, hired a moving van, then flew Ruth and her kids to California with me right after Christmas.

Now, I don't think I was nuts. Ruth and I were perfectly compatible. Her kids were cute. And I hadn't fallen this hard for a woman since my last long-term relationship three years before. I hadn't wanted us to drift apart the way a lot of commuter relationships do.

I was thrilled and enjoyed the shocked looks on my friends'

faces. My father squinted a little when I drove over my new brood to see him, but he was low-key about it. It was the most adventurous, romantic move of my life.

My ready-made family was terrific. The kids and I adored each other, and Ruth was terrific.

She found a job as a film editor, got the kids set for school, and I settled back into domestic bliss.

Around February my father called me and said that he had just had a strange conversation with Ruth. She had called to tell him that I was ruining her car, because I was a klutz with her stick shift. She wanted him to talk to me. This was odd, because I had my own car and had been driving a stick since I was sixteen. Dad and I decided that she must have just been making nervous conversation.

In April a friend of mine, a lawyer, came to town and spent a weekend with us. After he left, he called me and said he was alarmed by some questions that Ruth had asked him. She wanted to know how someone could prove senility, how to control the estate of someone who was mentally incompetent, and how money could be managed even if it was already accounted for in a will or trust. My friend said he thought she was referring to my father, who owned a lot of property, but I said he was wrong, and that I resented his accusations.

At the beginning of summer a female friend asked me to lunch and told me that she had run into Ruth in town, and that they had had a strange conversation. Ruth told her that she and her kids would be living with me only until she got settled and then would be leaving.

My friend must have misunderstood. Ruth and I were planning to get married. We had already discussed a Christmas wedding, and our home life was idyllic.

At the end of August I agreed to meet Lloyd for drinks one night, and when I got there, Lloyd was with four of my other friends. I felt as if they were beating me up. They had gotten together just to give me an earful on Ruth. She'd been telling my friends that I couldn't manage my affairs, and that I would have lost my job if she hadn't made me go to work. The clincher was when Lloyd said Ruth had told him that my father's senility was worsening and that he relied on her.

I lost my temper, chewed out my friends for trying to break Ruth and me up, and got in my car. Where did they get off trying to poison my relationship with her? They were still upset and worried that I had asked her to move in with me and had never really given her a full chance. They'd gone too far when they brought my father into it.

Truthfully, I would never have mentioned that night to Ruth, but when I got home, we had our first fight. She wanted me to swap cars with her and let her drive my new one, because she said I was blowing her engine when I shifted gears.

That triggered me. I told her everything I'd been bottling up inside, everything my friends had told me. Ruth denied it all, but once she started talking, she got confused, and denied statements of hers I hadn't even mentioned.

To test her, I told her that I wanted to move up the wedding. I wanted to get married next week, to be as spontaneous as we'd been before. She tried to weasel out of it, and without thinking, I told her to move out by the end of the month.

That's when she spun on me and said, "I'm not going anywhere. Do you think I'm a Ping-Pong ball and can uproot my kids at the drop of a hat because you're angry? If you don't want me around, then *you* can leave. You invited us to live with you, and we're all living here by agreement, so I'm not violating any law. California law says you can't kick me out, and you can't cut off any services in the house. You can't get us out of here unless we're the ones who want to leave. So make me get out."

She sat down and crossed her legs, looking calm. "You can

file a lawsuit, and I'll file a response, saying I disagree," she said matter-of-factly. "That'll tie you up for a couple of months until we get a court date. I can get free legal assistance in California because I'm a tenant, did you know that? So it won't cost me much to do whatever I need to do to keep you tied up in court and delay everything. I say you're looking at six months at best, but I think I can stretch it to a year. It's going to cost you money and time, and you're from around here, not me, so I hope you're ready for the public scrutiny. Or you can relax and sleep in the sunroom tonight. Got it?"

I got it. I'd gotten it good. Right where it counts.

She'd done her homework. If she couldn't get her hands on my father's trust, she'd get her hands on a house. Mine.

A few friends say that Ruth probably had this in mind since her first trip. I still prefer to think she moved here to be with me, and that this plan developed later.

It's a moot point, anyway, since I'm now living over the garage, and Ruth has had the house to herself for five months. Our only communication is the notes she tacks to my door, instructing me to get the lawn mowed or the house repainted. According to Lloyd, there is one saving grace to take comfort in: Now she has to buy her own groceries.

I'm working with a lawyer to get her out of my house, but it could take a while. In the meantime, life goes on, cautiously.

Tonight Lloyd called. He wanted me to get away and take a quick trip with him.

You know what I answered. I'm not taking any more cues or trips with my spontaneity guru for a long time. I'm not in the mood for any unexpected car-trip dates.

—Tommy, 35, computer systems analyst, California

I'd moped for months after my boyfriend dumped me, so several friends convinced me to go to a club with them. I went, knowing what the odds were for meeting a decent guy there—zilch.

I was standing at the bar when I heard a male voice ask if he could buy me a drink. Probably some reject. I turned to look at the person and thought, *Wow. What a hunk. He's probably married—or a psychopath.*

Turned out, he was more than normal, he was wonderful. Funny, smart, successful, and great-looking—tall, tan, with luxurious curly black hair and big brown eyes. And he seemed to be in great shape. We danced a few times and exchanged numbers. I knew I'd never see him again.

He called the next day, and we went out for the next two months, never doing more than kissing good night. My last boyfriend wasn't exactly handsome, so I was thrilled to be going out with a guy other women sneaked looks at. We talked all the time, finding out a lot about each other, even gaining each other's trust by being up-front about our past sex lives.

The big night arrived, and we kissed all the way to his bedroom. I was happy that we were going to make love. It was clear he was a great lover, and we were both revved to quite a pitch. Just as we got to the crucial moment, he said, "Hang on. There's one thing I have to do."

I said, "What's that?"

He reached up and tugged, and there was this dome head staring down at me, and his gorgeous, curly black hair dangling from his hand. It was a wig. He was as bald as a badger underneath.

—Joanne, 30, sales rep, Iowa

Usually I get up and go home as soon as I can. I give the woman a kiss, an "I'll call you," and I try not to make it obvious that I want to get out of her place as soon as I can. I'm your classic bad news guy. Do you know me?

Anyway, this woman is so fantastic, I have no desire to get out of her bed, even though it's dawn, my favorite time for a great escape.

I met her last night. I had been out with my buddies, having beers at a local bar. She had been out with her girlfriends.

We had both been standing at the jukebox, and I thought she was a dream—long red hair, great figure. She looked eighteen but claimed she was twenty-two. We both got bombed, and she and I left together and went to her apartment.

Let me put it this way: Xaviera Hollander, move over. This young woman has so many moves—what a repertoire—that she makes me seem like a boring old man. She's perfect. Not one thing wrong with her.

That's why I think I'll stay the morning. Or the week. Who knows? Maybe this is the time, once I find out her name, I'll even keep her phone number.

My hangover is killing me, and I need water. I squint open one eye and see a glass of water on the nightstand.

I sit up a little bit and bring the glass to my mouth, and I then can't stifle a yelp. My stomach starts churning.

Inside the glass are a full set of uppers and lowers. Teeth. *All* her teeth. I have no idea when she slipped them out.

—Russell, 29, manager, sporting goods store, Ohio

× × × × × × × × × × ×

We were kissing and really carrying on, if you get my drift. I had just met her that night, at a block party. I didn't live on her block—I was driving by, saw the party, and crashed it.

We were really going at it on the couch, and the front door opened. A man entered the room, said "Hello," then went upstairs.

That was weird, because both of us were in no condition for company. I tried to get up, but she had me pinned down.

"Who's that?" I asked her, trying to squirm out from under.

"Relax," she said, and pushed me back down. "That's my husband."

Who?

"Don't worry," she said. "His girlfriend is upstairs."

That was supposed to make me relax?

I said, "This is a wild house," and got up.

Whenever I tell this story, my best friend always asks me if I ever went back there, and I never answer him.

—Andrew, 25, real-estate broker, Connecticut

× × × × × × × × × ×

Imagine living in a swimming pool. I thought I could picture it. But the real thing was leagues beyond anything I envisioned.

I had made the mistake of telling my sister that I wanted to go out with a guy who didn't wear yellow neckties and pin-stripe suits. I'm an accountant, and I was tired of dating other accountants. My sister described Clark, a guy in her figure drawing class. Long black hair, big brown eyes, slim, medium height, ponytail.

"Cute," I'd said, picturing him. My sister had nodded.

On our blind date I met him at a coffee shop. I was expecting a sexy kind of guy, but sexy wasn't a word I'd use to describe Clark. He was dressed in all black, which is arty, but for some reason his ponytail looked affected, as if he'd be more comfortable in a crew cut. He was the palest person I'd ever seen, almost blue.

Our conversation was drifting along, neither charged nor flat. He told me that he had to show me his apartment, I kept refusing until he told me that he lived in a swimming pool. Fifteen years ago, he said, the apartment building he lived in had been a gym. He lived in the basement.

We drove our cars to his apartment building. Once inside the lobby, we bypassed the elevators and walked down a flight of stairs. He opened a door, flipped on a light, and motioned me in.

I wasn't prepared for the impact.

The space was gigantic, which it had to be, because the pool was nearly Olympic-size. Along the walls of the room huge paintings were stacked side by side. Each painting was of a bull's eye. Painting after painting of gray bull's-eyes, with black centers.

If there had been any cabana atmosphere around the pool, it was long gone. Exposed pipes were crammed on the ceiling. The same obsessive bull's-eyes even lined the walls of the pool.

"Have a drink," Clark said, motioning me from the deep end.

I walked down the wading steps, entering the shallow end, which was set up as his studio. At the five-foot mark, I was in the living room, complete with sofa and coffee table. The floor took a steeper slant, and I was in his kitchen. All the way at the deep end, was his bedroom. I looked up and could see the diving boards reaching over our heads.

I took my beer from him and asked him how the constant slant of the pool floor affected him.

"Must be weird to always see a slant, and always be on one," I said, so stunned I forget to be polite. All the furniture was on a slant, too; he hadn't built any platforms to create a straight floor.

"That's not a big deal," Clark said, sucking down his beer.

"It's the shin splints that'll get you. See?" He put down his beer can and lifted one of his pants legs.

Wrapped around one pale, hairy leg was an Ace bandage.

"I have to wear it almost all the time," he said. He came a little closer. "Better watch out. You don't want to get in over your head."

I think I actually sighed, which he probably misinterpreted as ecstasy. I wonder how many times he had tried out that stupid line.

I asked to use the bathroom, and he pointed.

I had to walk to the shallow end, get out, travel around the edge of the pool. Then I had to wind through the locker area until I found the four-stall ladies' room.

When I got back, he was bouncing on one of the diving boards. I looked into the pool. If he fell, he'd hit the concrete below.

"There's no water down there," I said.

"Am I scaring you?" he asked. "Are you worried about me? I'm used to this. I do it all the time. But one slip and—oh, no! Help!"

He was waving his hands and lifting one leg as if he might fall. I was afraid he might.

He got off the board and took my hand, leading me down the steps at the deep end, until we were standing on the floor of the pool, in his bedroom.

He kissed me, and I stared behind his head at the life preservers lining the wall.

He took off his jacket, and his shoulders poked up under his shirt. Without the shoulder pads, he was scrawny. I wondered if we weighed the same.

He pushed me, and we fell onto his bed, and even after we landed, I thought I was still falling, because the headboard was on the downhill side.

When he reached for my shirt buttons, I had this image of

being married to him, and having five kids, all of whom lived in the swimming pool and never saw light. We'd all be slightly blue, all our clothes would be gray, with one black dot on the center of our shirts, and we'd all limp around from shin splits.

I pushed him away. "No," I said, feeling clammy. "This won't work."

I thought about running to the shallow end, but it was all the way at the other end of the pool, so I climbed up the steel steps.

"I've got to go. Good night!" I called, walking past the lifeguard's station. "This is quite a place!"

He had climbed out of the deep end and was hobbling after me.

I didn't turn around, just waved over my shoulder and bolted up the stairwell until I was in the lobby, then raced onto the street.

I vowed, from then on, only to express interest in men who were periodontists, hard-hats, attorneys, or IRS investigators.

—Beatrice, 25, accountant, San Diego, California

× × × × × × × × × ×

We're in his bed, taking each other's clothes off. It's 2 A.M.

His phone rings, and thinking aloud, he says, "Should I get that? Or let my machine pick up?"

The phone and the answering machine are in his living room, which means he has to get out of bed.

We've had two previous dates that didn't lead to bed. He's a little shy. I like this guy a lot, and I want him in bed tonight. I vote for the answering machine and unzip his pants.

We're approaching the important moment, and the phone rings again.

He says, "I better get that," and I say, "Probably the wrong number. Forget it."

He worries for a second or two, and I distract him, but we've lost our momentum and essentially have to start over.

We're nearing the big moment again, and the phone rings again. He tries to get out of bed, but I hold him there.

The ringing stops.

I tell him I need a drink of water. On the way to his kitchen, I unplug one cord on his phone and plug the answering machine into the wall jack. Now his calls will get picked up on his machine, but the phone won't ring. I do this all the time at home.

The next morning he says, "Look at this! My answering machine says it took ten calls, but I didn't hear the phone ring that many times last night, did you?"

I say no, that it was either an incredible night—which it was, or his machine is on the blink.

"This must have come loose," I say, holding up a stray wire and readjusting the setup.

I'm in the shower, and I'm very happy. We're meeting again tonight, and he asked me to go away with him this weekend. I'm in love with this fellow.

He pulls back the shower curtain, and as I'm standing under the faucet with my eyes closed, rinsing soap off my face, he says, "That was my brother on the machine. My mother went into the hospital last night. He was trying to reach me so I could say good-by. She died at five A.M." Then he started crying.

Think my eyes popped open fast enough? Think I felt bad enough?

Think his mother's death was terrible enough? The horror didn't even end there. He wanted me to go to the hospital and funeral with him.

He thought that I burst into tears because I was so sensitive. He was trying to comfort me while he was sobbing.

I couldn't go with him. I had to go home and call one of those hot-line numbers, to see if they had some kind of advice on shame or guilt intervention.

I sent him a condolence card and included a letter explaining what I had done to his phone that night.

I told my friends that I couldn't blame him if he never called me again, but secretly I hoped he'd get over my stunt and call me. I thought there'd come a time when he'd put it behind him. Guess he never did.

—Kimberly, 32, paralegal, Maryland

× × × × × × × × × × ×

"Hey, Mommy! It's Tiny Tim! It's Tiny Tim!"

I tried not to hang my head in shame. My date did look like Tiny Tim. I've never hated the concept of blind dating more than I did that night. Everyone on the street did a double-take when they walked past me and my date, peering at him. If they got a good enough look at him, they stopped looking excited and would recoil. I've never walked so fast in my life.

It was July 13, 1977, and I'd been in New York City one week. I'd just gotten out of college and come up from Louisville, Kentucky. I didn't know one person, which is why I'd let one of my mother's Junior League friends set me up this blind date with a friend's son. It was my chance to get my social life going. I hadn't expected it to go down the tubes before it even got started.

Joe—my date—had picked me in the lobby of my apartment building, and my doorman had made a face when I got off the elevator and looked around the lobby for my date. Later, my doorman would explain that he was giving me "an assist": I should have taken a cue from the revolted look on the doorman's face and just kept walking—out the building.

Instead, the greenhorn I was, I walked right toward the guy and tried to wipe the nauseated look off my face.

Joe's hair was long, and it was filthy. Instead of the sweetness of Tiny Tim, this guy had a manicky look in his eyes, as if he'd just sucked down four gallons of coffee and was wired. He was drenched in patchouli oil.

We took two subways to our dinner destination—a coffee shop. Why did we have to go so far to eat at a basic diner? And, where in New York City were we? I had no idea. I'd left my map at my apartment. Joe was also twenty-two, and said he'd graduated in policial science, and felt he might want to become a transcendental meditation leader, but first he'd have to study TM. He smirked and said this career move might irk his dad, a lawyer who wanted Joe to go to law school.

The check came, and Joe ignored it. It occurred to me that going in and out of a trance would be a piece of cake for Joe.

"Should we split it?" I finally asked.

"Yes," he said, picking up the bill and studying it. "Even after the tip, the tax makes it come out to an odd amount. Who's going to pick up the extra penny?"

I said, "Me?"

He smiled and nodded.

We walked around the corner to a movie theater, and, once inside, I relaxed a little. It was a Woody Allen movie, and I was excited and proud that, for the first time, I was watching a movie about New York while I was in New York.

Joe lifted my hand off my lap and held it. I tried to tug it away from him, but he held on, and I gave up. What the heck, as long as that's all he wanted. I wanted to get back into the movie.

Then, there was the weirdest sensation. Familiar, yet creepy at the same time. I turned my head, and saw that he was sucking on my fingers.

I yelled, "Yuck!" and pulled my wet hand away, then jumped to my feet and left the movie.

Joe caught up with me, but I didn't say a word, even when he kept running along beside me, saying stupid things like "What are you so upset about? You're overreacting. Slow down. Let's get a drink. What's your problem?"

I ran down to the subway, praying my train would come so I could hop on it and ditch him. I was pacing the platform, trying to ignore him, when the lights went out. I could hear a huge generator grind to a halt somewhere close by.

Someone yelled, "Blackout!" and we all climbed the stairs up to the street.

"Better come with me until the power's restored," he said.

Like an idiot, I agreed.

What a surprise—Joe's apartment was only a block away.

It was a dump of a one-room apartment, with piles of newspapers, and a mattress on the floor that he pushed me onto.

He stood in front of me. My heart was thumping and I was terrified. I couldn't get any more naive or stupid.

Then he started singing—and playing air guitar.

"I'd strap on my guitar, but it's electric, and there's no juice, so why bother?" Joe asked, then went back to his strumming and singing. I finally paid attention to the words. He was singing about taking a girl's virginity, and punctuating his lyrics with simulated electric guitar whines at an ear-piercing level.

I got up, opened the door, and walked out. Joe never noticed. He was swinging his hair back and forth across his face, lost in a long solo.

—Amelia, 37, film production, Manhattan

4

Look who's sorry now . . .

No One to Blame But Yourself

Sometimes you simply have to shoulder the responsibility for your own dating fiascos.

Did you ignore that little voice in the back of your head that warned you from the very first instant that you were heading for trouble? Didn't your instincts go on red-alert when you accepted this date? (Did you *really* think your ex would set you up on a date with a winner?) Or worse, did you take a perfect golden opportunity and blow it?

One of my friends was the epitome of cool—so hip that she was on the "A" list at all the hottest clubs—and she was having a birthday celebration. First she was throwing a dinner party at her apartment, then we would head for a club.

After dinner I was going to meet Sam at the club. We'd

been introduced by mutual friends, and he was my first date since the crash of my four-year relationship six months earlier. I was nervous about the whole thing—the super-chic group and my date. I spent weeks agonizing over what to wear, hoping I looked cool enough. At the last second, to add some glamour, I switched from my usual flats to tall black heels.

I was so up-tight that I drank a lot of champagne at dinner. Then I got to the club and saw Sam. He was dancing with my friend Nancy—whom I knew he had a crush on. I was in such a rush to get to him that I slipped on my heels and fell the three steps that led to the dance floor, landing spread-eagle at the bottom. I peeled my face off the floor and wondered if I was making a hip impression yet. A few cool people turned around, and nonchalantly I announced, "Well, I think I just broke my foot."

My friends pulled me to a chair, and I asked them to find my date. By the time Sam got to me, my foot was swollen beyond recognition, on its way to looking like a football. I'd downed more champagne to cut the pain, and so I was drunk and not making much sense. He wanted to take me to a hospital, but I said, "I don't have to go, because my father is a doctor and I'm not like other people. I don't have to go to the hospital when something's wrong with me." I wanted my evening to start.

He said, "Your father can't fix your foot over the phone."

I said, "Yes, he can."

Sam suggested going to his apartment, which is across the street from a hospital, and we argued about staying at the club or going to his apartment, while I had more champagne. Finally I gave in.

Sam claims he made me call my father from his apartment, that my dad told me to go the hospital, and I argued with him. Then I hung up, saying, "I really don't have to go to the hospital. I refuse to go," and lay down on his couch and went to sleep.

I woke up at 6:00 in the morning, and my foot and head were throbbing. I shook Sam awake and said, "Sam. My foot's broken. I have to go to the hospital." So he carried me there.

I didn't see a doctor until 9 A.M. While I waited with Sam, he earnestly said, "Nina, I don't . . . I don't think I ever want to go out with you again."

I asked, "Sam, why?"

He told me that before I'd passed out, I'd said things to him like "I single-handledly ruined my ex-boyfriend's life."

I cringed and said, "Really? I actually said that?"

Then he told me that I had also said, "You shouldn't get tangled up with me. I'm totally bad news. I'll ruin your life. I'll take you from being a happy man and turn you into a quivering wreck."

After a pause I said, "Well, you've got a point."

—Nina, 27, accountant, Detroit, Michigan

× × × × × × × × × ×

Will and I ran to the two cots.

We didn't feel like sleeping. I was lying on my back, and I tossed back and forth, making my skirt spin from side to side.

I tossed again, and he laughed again. He was watching me and I was so happy! For months I'd wanted to sleep beside Will, and I finally got to.

Then Mrs. Gunter walked over and said to me, "Casey! I'm taking a star away from your name. Stop that. Will, stop laughing."

Then Will said, "Do it again, Casey. I like that."

I tossed, and he laughed again. I tossed two more times real fast, and Will was in convulsions.

"We're having fun together!" I said.

"Yeah," Will said. "Do it again."

"When I do that, I move so fast that I make you laugh," I said.

"No," Will said. "When you do that, I can see your underwear."

Then Mrs. Gunter called my name, and she took away another star for being noisy at nap time. Will rolled over and went to sleep.

—Casey, 5, kindergarten, Vermont

× × × × × × × × × ×

I lived in Houston, and the previous night I had seen the newscast about the woman being arrested for using a men's room. There I was one night later, of course, in a men's room.

It was an accident. Instead of being clearly labeled, the restaurant's bathroom doors had these indecipherable figures on the door. Torn between what looked like a cactus and some kind of a bird, I had gone with the cactus.

I had been in a rush and darted into a stall. Then I noticed that the place was filling up, and the feet in the stalls on either side of me were big shoes and large boots, and one pair was facing backward. Then the men started talking, and I got the picture.

I would just wait until it cleared out again and make a beeline for the bathroom door. I didn't want to get arrested.

I put my feet against the stall door so no one could see my shoes and waited. I waited ten minutes, and the boredom was horrible.

Then I thought I might scream: My date, Jeremy, was insecure about being stood up, and he had reason to be. The woman he had dated before me had ditched him at a concert, and he was still ragged around the edges from that. It had taken him months to ask anyone out after that. I was the first person he'd asked out since. He told me all this on our first date, and this was only our second. The timing wasn't good.

Every time I thought I could get out of there, another man or two would enter the room.

After twenty minutes I knew Jeremy was probably having flashbacks and hyperventilating into a paper bag, watching our appetizers congeal.

After thirty minutes I heard my name. Jeremy had come into the men's room. He had probably scoured the entire restaurant. I wanted to answer but didn't want to blow my cover, so I stayed quiet. I knew I'd be out any minute if I just stayed calm.

I was in there five more minutes before I got out and ran to our table. There was another couple in our chairs.

—Suzanne, 21, location scout, Houston, Texas

× × × × × × × × × × ×

When George asked me out, I almost keeled over. I'd had a crush on this guy for a year. I heard my mouth talking, and my brain hurried to catch up "Eight P.M.? Tonight? I don't get off work until midnight. I've got the late shift. I've just started these hours. The pharmacy might start being open twenty-four hours, so we're setting it up. But I'll probably still usually be free on Saturday night. What if we meet at twelve-thirty?"

I named the club, and George said okay, and that he'd never gone out on a date that started after midnight before.

The pharmacy had no plans to change its hours. I already had a date for the night. I wasn't at all excited about that date, but I was still in that stage where any date was better than no date at all.

I had never double-booked dates before, that's how much I wanted to go out with George. I tried to call my original date and cancel, but he wasn't home. Rather than panic, I decided I'd take things one step at a time, and I'd be fine. I could be home by midnight, and in my car by 12:15.

My date took me to a party, and I watched the clock. When he wasn't looking, I'd empty my drink and bring us each a fresh one. I fed him a stiff bourbon every half-hour. I felt evil, but I rationalized that I was just a Saturday night fill-in for him, too. At 11:30 he was engrossed in a game of throwing a Smurf doll through a NERF-ball hoop. He was so drunk that he was walking right by me and not even noticing who I was.

At midnight I wandered to the front of the house and caught a ride from the party to my apartment. Then I drove to the club.

I was fifteen minutes late, but George didn't mention it. We danced and talked, and I forgot about my first date until George said, "There's nothing fishy about tonight, is there? Because I went by the pharmacy around eleven, and no one was there. Do you have a boyfriend or something? I don't want to get caught in a scene like that."

I told him I didn't have a boyfriend, and that I had been doing inventory in the back of the store with another pharmacist; we didn't answer the door because people would want us to fill prescriptions.

He said, "No game playing, right?"

I said, "No game playing. I hate that."

At 2 A.M., dancing to a slow tune, I heard, "Bet you didn't think I'd sober up, did you?"

My first date of the night had shown up with friends. George and I stopped dancing, and I chewed my gum furiously, trying to think of a way out of this mess.

"At first I felt kind of bad that I got so drunk," my party date said, "then I figured out that you'd gotten me loaded. 'Cause everyone said, funny thing, you were stone sober. Real clever. Yeah, so I go by your place, and your car is gone, so I just drove from one bar to another until I found you. Thought you gave me the slip, right? If I'm your date, who's this?"

Well, that was a good question. I could say I wandered in, and he asked me to dance, and I didn't know him before this one dance. George would back me up.

George said, "If I'm your date, who's this?"

—Vanessa, 31, pharmacist, Indianapolis, Indiana

× × × × × × × × × ×

Eric's integrity was legendary with his friends. I met him at a party. When I asked our mutual friend for the low-down, she said, "He never lies, he helps out everybody, never says anything negative about anyone. Can you stand it?" Add that to the fact that he was a knockout, successful, and popular, and he was one in a million.

We'd been dating for a month. I'd spent Friday night at his house with him, and the next morning he went to his office to do some work. Before he left, he said he'd be back at 6:00, and asked if I could meet him back at his house around then. He kissed me, put a set of keys in my hand, and said, "These are yours."

Keys! And a Friday-through-Sunday with him! This was serious! I was flying.

I took a shower, made a cup of coffee, and realized it was the first time I was alone in his apartment.

I roamed around in my towel, combing my hair, then sat at his desk, playing with his pens. I opened a drawer. Inside were snapshots of a gorgeous woman on a beach. I put them on the desk and rummaged through the other drawers. I discovered a box of photos and letters, all posted from the same out-of-town address.

I grabbed my glasses and the box and sat on the floor. I found photos of him with her. I started reading the letters. I couldn't tell if they had dated in the past, which could mean he was still carrying a torch for her, or if it was current.

One section in a letter slayed me: "Are you still glad I'll be transferred? Can't believe my boss gave in. Can't believe we'll finally be living in the same zip code. Don't worry about boredom setting in, because I'm never going to get frumpy, and we'll make love every day or twice a day (or three times a day, or four times a day)."

I hated her. Her letters made me sick. She sounded as if she were an advanced teenager. And she was disorganized. Why didn't she date her letters? And why didn't he save all the envelopes? This was going to be a nightmare, figuring out if she was past or present. But I was also excited by my discovery of her and by the prospect of solving the mystery of who she was. I held up a picture of her in a bikini. She was in good shape, which irked me, but she could use a good haircut.

Then I found a letter that sounded the most recent. I found a clue! She was history. She never moved. And either she lost interest, or he did, because the letter had that "Well, old buddy" tone to it. I'd done it! I'd solved the mystery. My relationship was safe! I leaned back, grinning, because I'd been so worried.

Eric was standing in the doorway to the room, his arms folded, and a blank look on his face.

How could I have pulled that situation out of the trash? How could I act nonchalant, sitting in the middle of his floor in a bath towel, wearing glasses, all his desk drawers open, his love letters strewn around me? The only thing I hadn't done was dust the house for prints.

I got dressed, handed him the keys, and he held the door open for me.

—Ruby, 36, political consultant, Atlanta, Georgia

× × × × × × × × × × ×

Money is important to me. Shoot me. Think less of me. I don't care. Just don't set me up on a blind date with a struggling guy. Set me up with his rich father.

This European zillionaire was suitable blind-date material. He was into everything: diamonds, planes, propane. He was even a humanitarian, on the boards of several nonprofit organizations. He told me he loved those endeavors the most, working with everything from the environment to charities.

His dinner conversation was entertaining. A little heavy on bravado about himself, but I could live with that.

On our way into a bar for a drink, he shouted to a man who approached him with his hand out, "Get a job! Get going! If you can hit me for a quarter you can stand in line for a job. What's scum like you doing on the street? You can't even pick up the trash on the corner you're panhandling on! You make me sick! What's your problem?"

"His problem is, he's homeless," I said, dragging my zillionaire into the bar. "He's one of the people you're supposed to feel compassion for."

My date was just drunk. Perhaps he'd had some traumatic panhandling experience. You never know. Who was I to pass judgment? The guy had a platinum charge card.

The singer at the bar, a pretty brunette, opened her set by asking, "Please do me a favor, everyone, and don't smoke. I'm recovering from a brochial condition."

Well, I smoke, so that was going to be a problem for me, but I could manage to live through a few smoke-free songs before I went outside and lit up.

My date immediately yelled, "Watch this, honey!" and lit a cigarette.

I asked, "Aren't you on the board of a health group? Isn't it a lung association?"

He looked at me as if I were speaking a foreign language and said, "No, it's one of the other ones. One of the other organs. Hey, honey! Can you sing 'When I Think of You, I Touch Myself'?"

Well, it's a great song. By the diVINYLS. But my date was laughing like a loud hyena. Apparently he didn't appreciate the song so much as wanting to embarrass the singer.

He opened his wallet. "Sweetheart," he practically yelled to me, "want to hold this?" and held up his platinum credit card. I wondered if he'd seen me eying it earlier. "Just kidding!" he said. "That was a joke! Want to hold it, anyway?"

I sat there for twenty minutes, while he got drunker and yelled semi-obscene requests to the singer.

As we were leaving the bar, the same street person said, "You again! You're disgusting!"

My zillionaire said, "Me? *You're* disgusting."

I watched them bicker back and forth: "*You're* disgusting."—"No, *you're* disgusting."

After a few rounds of this, I told my date we should go.

He said, "Hold on a minute. Hey, buddy—*you're* disgusting."

The homeless man said, "No, *you're* disgusting."

My feeling was, the street man had a point.

A taxi rounded the corner, and I got in it without saying good night to my date. He didn't notice, caught up as he was in his complex debate.

Money couldn't make the man, it was true. Money couldn't even make the night bearable. When I found myself thinking that that homeless man might be cute if he got cleaned up, I realized that I was having financial mood swings. I had some reappraising of financial standards to do. Somewhere between zillionaire and homeless is a lot of territory, and a lot of opportunity.

—Lillie, 29, loan processor, New Orleans, Louisiana

× × × × × × × × × × ×

Crystal? A guy with no priors (translation: no previous marriages) who has his own crystal glasses and decanters?

Jeff is the best date I've had in a long time. He owns an art gallery, is intelligent, distinguished looking, and polished. So polished that I feel a little insecure. I edit the horoscope and advice columns for a small newspaper, so Jeff seems out of my league. We're having a drink at his house before he takes me to dinner, and he's poured us both something that tastes like licorice. It's very good.

He's precise about everything. While he's talking or listening, he straightens out the blue cocktail napkins, arranging them perfectly parallel to the edges of the coffee table. He flicks a stray cheese crumb from the table. As we're leaving, Jeff realigns his crystal glasses on the shelf, making sure the rows are precise. He runs a lint brush over his jacket and offers it to me, but I decline. I'm on a date with Felix Unger, and I'm a little afraid that I'm the Oscar Madison part of this odd couple.

Things are going beautifully at the restaurant—a very posh French restaurant where the prices are sky-high, and there's an expensive hush over the patrons. If I owned a tiara, this would be the place to wear it.

Jeff's a great guy, but what a neatness freak. He's sent back both sets of our silverware because he said they didn't look clean enough, and the wine barely passes his taste test. Talk about finicky. Our lamb entrees are overcooked for him, though mine seems raw to me, and he sends those back, too. To my surprise, the waiter is embarrassed and apologetic. But it's worth the wait. Dinner is great, and the conversation is lovely.

Over our dessert and coffee, he stops midsentence and says, "Enough about me. Let's talk about you. What do *you* think about me?"

I burst out laughing. Jeff hasn't monopolized the conversation at all, but it's a funny line, and I can't stop laughing.

Then I can't stop choking. I'm choking on a bite of his cake I've just sampled—like the mousse I polished off wasn't enough. He's been laughing along with me, and while he's watching my face, he starts to mimic my choking expression and then looks alarmed and says, "Are you okay?"

I don't know. I pour water down my throat, but it comes right back up, and I spray it across the table.

I start pointing to my throat, gasping, and feel lightheaded. I'm having trouble breathing, and I can't talk. I grab my neck.

Jeff leaps to his feet, pulls me to mine, and puts his arms around me from behind, attempting the Heimlich Maneuver.

"Don't worry!" he yells excitedly, "I saw this on Channel Two."

He is squashing my ribs, and I feel like they are going to crack.

I hear the couple at the next table say, "Another choker. This is happening to us again."

Then I hear a woman yell, "Your hands are too high! Lower your hands!"

A man yells, "A quick sharp jab, not a bunch of little nudges!"

Everyone is shouting tips, and Jeff is swinging me around as he turns in the direction of the helpful hints.

I don't care, because I'm fading fast. There's a detached quality to everything that's happening.

Jeff lets go of me, and a woman takes over. I'm facing him, thinking, "I finally get a decent date, and I choke to death. So long, you knockout."

In one jab, I feel life return, and I barely hear the applause. I do see Jeff's face. I've thrown up all over him.

—Lydia, 53, newspaper editor, Illinois

× × × × × × × × × ×

These two sisters were the kind of women that men melt over. They were good-looking, but there was something wild about them that made men go brain dead. They were hypnotizing, and rumor had it they were trouble with a capital *T*.

This was back in 1956, and I was thirty. It's a two-part story, you see, because I was out of my mind about both of them.

I decided to start out with Paula, the less wild of the two. I asked her out every other day for three weeks, and she refused every time, which was very peculiar, because women used to throw themselves in front of my car to get a date with me.

Finally Paula said, "Tell you what. My friends and I are having a party next Saturday. Why don't you come? You can be my date."

Bingo. I asked what her favorite drink was, and she said whiskey. So I bought new clothes, and I had a case of primo whiskey sent to her house for the party.

On the way to the party I picked up a bottle of the best champagne I could find and drove over to her place. The house was dark, but I pumped the doorbell. I figured the party was out back, so I walked around to her backyard, but no one was there, either. Can you believe that? She had given me the wrong date. The party was the night before, and she had thought I'd stood her up.

My brother, who was also hot for these girls, would tell you that Paula moved the party to someone else's house and they drank all my whiskey, just to spite me. His theory is she wanted to teach me a lesson for hitting on her all the time. Keep in mind, of course, that he wasn't invited to the party, so he's still touchy about that.

Well, I kept hitting on Paula, and she kept saying she couldn't go out with a guy who stood her up, and so I got tired of telling her she had it all wrong, so I moved on to her sister, Judy. Whoa, was *she* something. She was a pistol, and she had a walk that you couldn't believe, nothing showy, just some slight hip action that could make you stagger.

I wanted to impress this gal, so I invited her to Mexico. And she said, "Let's go." I had expected her to string me along, but she was obviously waiting for me to ask her out. We were going to Monterrey on Saturday, so on Thursday I bought this turquoise Thunderbird convertible—beautiful.

I picked her up Saturday morning, and she bragged on the car, and things were going real good. We were driving along, and she was playing with my neck and kissing me. Things were going so good that I feel like a young man just thinking about it. So good that when we crossed the border heading for Monterrey, I figured that was far enough. She was ready, I was ready.

I pulled into the first motel I could find, and she was getting hotter and hotter while we were checking in.

Then we got to the room and I closed the door and said we should get in bed, and she said, real sweet, "That sounds good, Roy. Why don't you take the first shower."

I said okay.

I was in the shower, whistling and humming. When I came running out of the shower, the room was empty. Empty of Judy, of my clothes and my shoes and my car keys and my suitcase and my wallet. She left me some cash, though.

I had to call a motel clerk to see if I could figure out in Spanish if I had enough money to buy clothes and shoes and get back home. It was too late at night to get clothes, or to get a bus out of there. And I didn't have enough money to order anything but a *burrito* and wait until morning.

I finally got back to town—I took a bus that had stopped at every little one-horse town and cactus patch.

My car was in my carport, along with my clothes and keys and wallet. I called Judy, and you know what she said? She said she was in over her head with me, and that she could marry me, except she'd just gotten a divorce and wasn't ready to settle down so quick. She asked me to wait.

I waited a couple of days and started calling her again, but she never went out with me.

You can imagine my brother's version of all this. That those two women were tired of me and ran me through the wringer for the fun of it. Course, he never got Judy to start out for Monterrey with him, and I did.

—Roy, 65, café owner, Corpus Christi, Texas

× × × × × × × × × ×

One day, as I cut across the middle of Fifth Avenue and jumped onto the curb, a man said, "Do you always jaywalk?" I ignored him but noticed that he was extremely attractive and well dressed. Not your typical street hassler.

He fell in step with me, and we started talking. I mentioned that I work in computers, and it turned out that he had a good friend who worked in another department at my company. This guy didn't work himself, just traveled, which made sense when he hinted that his father had been a Wall Street tycoon before the 1987 crash. There was something appealing about his manner, and when he asked for my business card, I was happy to give it to him. We had the mutual acquaintance at my company, and unless he was lying, he seemed to be from a good family. It was not a high-risk situation.

He called at work the next day and wanted to meet immediately for drinks. I thought that was odd, considering it was only 2:00, and suggested meeting that evening. He chose the place—a posh, cozy midtown bar.

I thought it was peculiar that he was wearing the same clothes he'd had on the day before, but then he complained about the garage where he had just parked his Porsche, and I relaxed. When he smiled, there was a gleam in his eyes that I found intriguing—something devilish.

I enjoyed his company, except that he was drinking like a fish, which made me uneasy. He'd had four drinks in an hour and a half, and was ordering an array of the best appetizers, including caviar. I was nervous every time he ordered another drink, but then he'd tell me a hysterical story, and I'd think he was charming.

At 1:00 in the morning, I didn't think he was so charming any more; he was loud and sloppy-drunk. It sounded like he said, "You're about fifteen pounds overweight, but I think you're kind of pretty, anyway," but he was slurring his words, so I wasn't sure. He became agitated every time I suggested calling it a night, and I was worriedly trying to think of a way out that wouldn't provoke a scene.

It was getting late, and the bar was closing. My date fumbled with his pockets, saying, "I'm out of cash. Can I borrow ten dollars for cigarettes?" That was odd, but cigarettes could be expensive in fancy bars, and he probably wanted to be prepared. I gave him the money, which was all the cash I had. He said he'd be right back.

After he'd left, two couples at the next table leaned toward me, and one of the women said, "How well do you know that guy?"

What could I say—"Met him on the street!"? It was humiliating. So I told her I'd known him a long time. Her friends ignored my answer and asked me a barrage of questions like "Is it a blind date?" "Who set you up?" The last question was a blow: "You know he's not coming back, don't you?"

No, I didn't. There was no way he would ditch me. They were leaving and wanted to give me some money, and I felt awful that strangers thought I was pathetic. I turned them down.

After twenty minutes I went to the back of the bar, but my

date wasn't there. A busboy said the men's room was empty. I sat back down, waited another fifteen minutes, and looked at his chair. His jacket was gone—he'd taken it with him when he went for cigarettes. No sense denying it any more. I had been ditched.

I was the last customer of the night. The waiter handed me the bill, and I felt the room spin. Two hundred dollars. The guy was devilish, all right. I gave the waiter my charge card and put my head in my hands. I couldn't understand how this could be happening to me.

The waiter said my charge card had been refused. Turned out it had expired the day before and I'd left the new card at home. I had a vision of being handcuffed and tomorrow's front-page news. I said, "I can't pay the bill. I don't have the money." I was too dazed to be tactful. The waiter went away and came back with a security guard.

I explained the whole story, and the guard and the waiter both asked, "How well did you know him? Were you fixed up?" Everyone kept asking the same questions. Finally, I convinced them to call my roommate and verify that I was who I said I was. They asked me to leave all the identification I had and to come back in the morning with cash.

I thanked them and left, raised my arm to flag a cab, and then realized: I didn't have any cash.

Some date. Who knew who he really was? Not only had he left me with the bill, he'd left me doubting my judgment and with a taste of what being victimized was like. I would have to walk the two miles home alone at 3:00 in the morning. The whole way I had the same childhood memory, my parents' voices saying, "Don't talk to strangers. No matter how nice they seem." No kidding.

—Barbara, 25, software analyst, New York, New York

× × × × × × × × × × ×

"I should warn you," she says on the phone. "I have really tight lug nuts."

This is a turnon for me. Don't ask me why. I have no business even talking to her for long on the phone. I certainly have no business accepting a date with her. Shannon has just stopped dating my roommate, Jim, and Jim is a psychopath. He's a Ted Bundy type and looks a lot like him—handsome and mean. The icing on this cake is that Jim is also a judo expert.

My car is in the shop, and we'll have to take hers. But first I have to fix her flat tire.

Jim isn't home, so I call my father to talk this over. "Yeah, I like her," I answer my father about Shannon. "And I'm flattered she called and asked me out. It's to some party. But Jim is gonna be furious. On the other hand, I have to live my own life. And Shannon's not Jim's property. I think I should go with her, and be up-front with Jim."

My father's advice is "Okay."

Jim is surprisingly calm when he comes home and I tell him about my date that night with Shannon.

"I'm going to the same party," Jim says, "with my own date, anyway. So it's no big deal for me. I'm glad you told me."

That was easy. What had I been worried about?

I take a bus to Shannon's house, and find out she's right: I have a heck of a time changing the tire. I remember how much I hate to change flats, and I realize that our date is starting off with an unmistakable reminder of Jim (also known as the Terminator). Only he could have put these lug nuts on so tight. Maybe Shannon won't notice what a weakling I am compared to him.

We get to the party, and things are going smoothly until 1 A.M. That's when Jim, who is looped, drives back to the party after taking his date home. Shannon is looped, too, and they go outside and start to argue, eventually screaming back and forth about each other's faults. Shannon throws a soda bottle at Jim, and he throws a soda can at her.

I still consider Shannon my date, and not Jim's, but haven't seen a safe opening, so I stay indoors with everyone else, watching the fight.

Three women coax Shannon inside, and I watch the fireworks when the host tells Jim that he has found Jim's car keys inside, and that he isn't going to let Jim drive home.

"You've had too many beers," the host bravely says. "You'll wind up in a car wreck. Get a lift."

I never could have guessed that Shannon and I would be the lift, but we are, by default, being some of the last to leave.

Jim insists on driving Shannon's car, and Shannon insists on sitting in the front so she can watch him drive, and she also insists I sit between them.

I oblige, hoping to head off more fireworks.

I yell to Jim to slow down, but he doesn't hear me, because he and Shannon are yelling over my head.

As we're coming to a stop at Shannon's house, Jim pulls out a gun and starts shooting it in the air, which in this case means through the roof. Shannon starts trying to hit Jim, I fend her off for him and I yell to Jim to put down his gun and get out of the car.

When he says he won't, I tell Shannon to get out of the car, and she won't.

I'm stuck between a judo expert with a gun and his livid ex-girlfriend.

I look at Jim and shout, "Do you still like her?"

Jim yells, "Of course I do."

I yell at Shannon, "Do you still like him?"

She yells, "I hate him!" and tries to stand up on the seat to swat him.

That's enough for me. She's crazy about him, he's crazy

about her—they're both crazy, period. Besides, Jim has just told me, "Earl, I feel like pounding you silly."

I'd like to leave them in the car together, but I have to get out first, so I lean across Shannon and open the door, then push her out and follow her.

Jim shoots his gun through the roof again, and I tell him, "I'm getting Shannon inside, then I'm going to the corner to call a friend to come get me. You go home, and call Shannon tomorrow."

Shannon says she's not going inside until Jim apologizes for ruining her date and the roof of her car. I can see that that's beyond Jim's capacity, and I can see that if I leave her outside, all hell will break loose.

I say, "You *will* go inside. I've had my fill of this," and I pick her up and carry her to her door. Her roommate opens the door, and I tell her roommate, "When I put her down, lock the door, and don't let her go outside."

I put her down, slam the door, and run away from the car, headed for a convenience store.

Jim drives slowly by the store, but he doesn't stop.

I don't think it's safe to go home tonight, so I call my father, tell him what happened, and ask for a lift and if I can sleep over.

I can tell my father is mulling over all this and probably has something to say.

My father says, "Okay."

I shouldn't have gone out with Shannon, and shouldn't be living with Jim, and I should have read between the lines when Shannon told me the line that hooked me on the date. Tight lug nuts are always trouble.

—Earl, 27, carpenter, Illinois

× × × × × × × × × ×

It's funny how misty-eyed you can get over old high school or college friends. Whether you liked, barely knew, or despised them, if you see them after a long time has passed, it's like coming home again.

Running into Ted at a Honolulu hotel had been strange. For one thing, we hadn't seen each other since we'd dated in college at Duke. For another thing, sex had always been a big issue for us, though I had trouble remembering why. Some of the sexual tension was still there, though.

I live in Honolulu now, and he still lives in North Carolina. I was at the hotel to have lunch with a doctor I used to work with, and he was staying there on business. After we hugged, he asked me to meet him for dinner.

Dinner was fun, gossiping about old pals. Ted was married and pulled out an accordion file of photos, featuring his kids and wife. I showed him a photo of my boyfriend.

As dinner was ending, he said, "What kind of birth control do you use? I bought condoms on the way over just in case."

Then I remembered. All those nights of arguing. I had liked Ted, but not enough to sleep with him, and that had driven him nuts. He knew I had slept with other men in college, just not with him. Aside from the fact that I wasn't that attracted to him physically, he was a bigmouth about sex and always went into graphic detail with his buddies about what he did in bed with the woman, what she did, how long it had taken.

"Forget it," I said. "You're married."

"It's fourteen years later," he said. "Time for you to give in. Let's do it."

I said no, and we argued for ten minutes.

Suddenly Ted stood up and yelled my full name, then yelled, "You're having sex with me tonight if it kills you. Now get up, and let's go."

He still has a big mouth.

—Julie, 36, surgeon, Honolulu

× × × × × × × × × × ×

I'm not really a boxer, but here I am, my first time in the ring, getting beat up.

I'm the night bartender in this little resort town, and in winter, business slows to a trickle, and there isn't much to do. One of my regular customers is a boxer. There are fifteen guys on the team he's with. He invites me to train with him when I'm not at work, and I'm so bored I think it's a great idea.

He trains eight hours a day, and I train with him for four, spending time at his gym and learning moves in the ring. I had been a blob, but by the end of the year, I'm fit.

The coach of the boxing team has three good-looking daughters, and they're going through the team three at a time, then moving on to the next three guys. The guys on the team haven't figured this out, because none of them knows about it. They aren't talking about sleeping with these girls, because they know if they gossip to one another, and the word gets back to the coach that they're banging his daughters, first the coach'll beat them up, then he'll throw them off the team. I only find out because one of the daughters hangs out at the bar a lot, and she spills the beans about the whole thing—to me. She tells me I've become one of her closest friends, and I'm touched, because I don't have many friends up here. I should probably discourage her, but since we're on the up-and-up platonic, I let the friendship take root.

The coach has arranged for our team to fight another team. I didn't think I'd be in the ring for a year—or ever. But the coach tells me I'm ready, and I'm fighting another featherweight, named Rex. Mine's the last fight, on Friday.

Fight week I watch every single match. The other team is killing us. It's not that they're so much better. It's that the coach's daughters have been wearing out our team.

On Friday I'm ready for Rex. Except, Rex doesn't show. He's sick, so I get his big brother, Rubin. I weigh 125 pounds, Rubin is around 170. He's a light heavyweight. I'm supposed to go four three-minute rounds with this guy

I hightail it to the coach and say, "Coach! What's going on? That son of a bitch is gonna *kill* me."

Coach says, "Remember to circle to his right."

I go to the center of the ring, Rubin and I match gloves, and I tell Rubin, "You're gonna *kill* me."

The bell rings, I circle to his right, and the lights nearly go out, and my intestines almost take the express bus to my throat. A black eye is on the way, and I feel a couple of ribs buckle on my right side.

At the end of the round I gasp to the coach, "He nearly beat the shit out of me, Coach. Help me!"

Coach says, "Circle to his right."

The bell rings for the second round. I circle to Rubin's right, and I don't see it coming, but I do feel more ribs crack on my left side.

At the end of the round I say, "Coach, do you see that guy killing me?"

Coach says, "Stick with my advice. Circle to his right."

Right about then I decide I'd better start circling left.

I hang in the third round by circling left and by using some strategy; I fall against the ropes and spring back to get some extra force going, and pop Rubin in the face. This seems to work. I wonder if I can keep it up in the fourth, or if Rubin will figure out a way to get around me.

At the end of the round I stumble to my corner and say, "I'm not sleeping with your daughter, Coach!"

Coach looks at me hard, then says, "Circle left."

I was getting the hell beat out of me because of dates with his daughter that I never even had.

That was my first and last pro fight, and it ended in a draw for me, Rubin—and Coach. I don't think he ever completely believed me.

—Josh, 20, bartender, California

× × × × × × × × × × ×

His nickname is Disaster Derek. Wherever he goes, disaster follows most of the time. Once he entered a restaurant, and before he was seated, the kitchen had a major fire. He visited a friend and the police stormed in, busting the wrong house by mistake. He went snow skiing with a girlfriend, they got separated at the lift line, and hers was the only chair that broke off the cable and fell—four feet, but hey. . . .

His friends tell me these stories. Derek and I have been dating for six months, and nothing odd has happened. Either his luck has changed, or his friends make up those stories and Derek just plays along, enjoying being an odd celebrity.

It's Thursday night, and we're driving from Las Cruces, New Mexico, to Juárez, Mexico, for dinner. It's a pretty short hop—and we're taking my Land Cruiser. Except, it won't start. Derek says we'll take his car, and my instinct is to say no, because it's a standard and I can't drive a stick, but as I always do when I experience intuition, I ignore it and get into Derek's car.

We cross into Mexico with no problem and find a casual place to have dinner. Derek starts ordering shots of tequila. The people at the next table are from Las Cruces, too, and soon Derek and I are sitting at their table, and we're all doing shots. I do a couple, but they do so many that I lose count.

They invite us to their hotel room, and Derek accepts. I stop drinking, but Derek now has his own tequila bottle and keeps working on it until he stops being unnaturally rowdy and cocky about eating the worm in the bottle, and passes out.

Derek weighs 220, and we leave him on the floor. I sleep next to him, along with two other people.

The next morning, I call my office and lie about having to visit a friend in the hospital. The Las Cruces gang helps me get Derek into the back seat of the car. I wave and turn the key, and the car stalls.

I try to get Derek to perk up, but he's green and semi-conscious. One of his drinking buddies gets in and says he'll give me a quick driving lesson. We lurch and stall around the hotel, and after twenty minutes I have to drop him off.

I'm on my own, lurching my way to the border, the engine dying every five minutes. I can see the border checkpoint, and I know we're almost home free. I get in line behind the other cars. Just as it's my turn to pull up, a guard puts a barricade in front of the stall. He puts up a hand and shouts that he'll be right back, but my car lurches and crashes the barricade, and this time it doesn't stall.

I push the barricade ten feet, still can't find the brake, and still can't get the car even to stall.

I hear the siren behind me and slam on the break but hit the clutch instead. The car jolts to a stop just in time. A patrol car has done a ninety-degree turn in front of me and has me blocked off. Good thing I don't crash that, too.

At least I'll be booked on the U.S. side of the border.

—Michelle, 40, physical therapist, Las Cruces, New Mexico

× × × × × × × × × × ×

Try getting a date during World War II if you think it can be tough now.

My friend Marjorie wanted a date—she hadn't had one in more than a year. So when my beau, Lyle, was on leave from the Navy in New York, I asked him if he had a friend for Marjorie. Knowing Lyle had poor judgment in people, often gravitating to people for the wrong reasons, I gave him the parameters of tall, smart, reasonably nice looking. I figured that guidance would guarantee Marjorie a decent date, wouldn't challenge Lyle with an impossible standard, and wouldn't give him too much room for a mistake. He called back and said he had just the guy, and we set up our double date.

Lyle's friend was around five foot ten. He was horrible looking, but a winning personality could have overshadowed his appearance. Looks aside, he pinched our waitress's derriere, then asked if he could take his shoes off. Marjorie said no, but he did. The odor was horrendous, causing us to gag. He and Lyle made jokes about his feet being a secret weapon.

Marjorie and I had never met anyone so stupid. He explained to us that the subway was useless in New York City. He held forth at great length about how night invasions would be better during the day, because the enemy would be taken by surprise. Lyle nodded along, which was surprising, because he was a very bright man.

If only Marjorie's date had been stupid but attractive, or bright but an eyesore. Or hideous and dumb but polite.

The climax of the night was when he pretended to sneeze directly onto all of our desserts and thought that was so funny he did it again.

That was the last straw. Marjorie and I said good night to the men.

Lyle called that night, truly baffled by why we had left. I asked him how he could have brought along such a cretin for Marjorie, and he said, "Oh, that's easy. I'm broke, and he's the only guy on our ship who has money. What's the problem?"

—Carlotta, 68, seamstress, New York City

× × × × × × × × × ×

"Guess!" Bart practically begs me.

"I don't want to," I say, feeling queasy.

"Come on, guess!" Bart says again.

We're at a coffee shop in Houston. Bart has driven in to see me.

I'm finishing my summer internship at an architect's firm, and next week I'll be going home and back to college in Louisiana. This will be the last year of school for me and Bart. We dated all year, and it was tough being separated this summer. Bart didn't have an internship, so he stayed in Louisiana with his family. He drove in to see me one other time, which might not seem like much, but we've kept in touch with phone calls twice a week. I'd been so busy at work that I'd discouraged trips to see each other. It had been a big summer for me, and I knew Bart and I loved each other enough that we didn't always have to act like love birds.

He had shown up at my office unexpectedly, wearing a suit, which I thought was highly romantic. He looked wonderful—handsome and happy. My colleagues kept sneaking me winks, and my boss told me to take the rest of the day off.

I wanted to go to my apartment, but Bart said he had an announcement that couldn't wait. I imagined a diamond solitaire and took him to a coffee shop around the corner from my office.

"I will!" I had blurted out, feeling giddy and in a teasing mood.

"You'll what?" Bart had asked.

"I'll . . . have some coffee," I said, playing along, pretending I didn't know what was up. "What's your announcement?"

"I'm in love with one of your girlfriends," Bart said. He was always direct. "We've been seeing each other since you left, and we're getting engaged."

"Who . . . is it?" I asked, feeling KO'd. In all the calls and letters from my friends, no one had mentioned a romance.

That's when Bart says, "Guess! Go ahead. Just guess!"

I don't want to, but I realize that Bart is so pleased that he kept it secret, and so pleased that he's in love and can tell me about it, that he won't ruin the surprise by just telling me. If I want to find out, I've got to ask.

"Maddie," I say, suddenly feeling tired.

"No!" Bart looks triumphant. "Try one of your best friends."

"Kristin."

"No! But you're getting warmer."

"Angela?"

"No! Now you're getting cold!"

"Lee?"

"Warmer! This is really an interesting way to find out, isn't it? Isn't this kind of fun?"

—Joanie, 21, architect-in-training, Louisiana

× × × × × × × × × ×

On again, off again. I'd dated like that for years. For some reason I always found myself hooked on those relationships. Ex-girlfriends were as interesting to me as a new girlfriend most of the time.

I ran into her at a party the year after college, and we raced back to her apartment to get in bed. We burned up the sheets that night. She was cooing love words in my ear, and I was cooing them back. We didn't sleep at all. At sunup, we took a shower together. As we were toweling each other off, she said, "I can't see you any more."

This didn't faze me. Once she was through with a new boyfriend and I was through with a new girlfriend, she and I would be dating and back in bed again. This was round four for us.

"Why not?" I asked, waiting for her to go through the rigmarole of "I met this guy, and . . ."

She said, "I'm getting married tomorrow."

For once in my life I was speechless.

—Ian, 22, deejay, Birmingham, Alabama

× × × × × × × × × ×

Sean had selected me from a video dating service, and when he called he told me how much he liked me in my video—especially liked my reply to what I wanted most in a date. My reply had been "sincerity." It had just slipped out. I wanted to come up with an answer that might be more unusual. He'd fallen for it.

We had a nice chat, and arranged to meet for an early dinner after work the next night.

At the office the next afternoon, it was my boss's birthday, and the department threw a party for her. I drank two or three glasses of champagne and was light-headed by the time I got to the restaurant to meet my date.

I was first to arrive, so I sat at the bar, ordered a glass of champagne, and glanced around. I was having my usual blind-date thoughts such as, *I hope he pays . . . What if he's grotesque? . . . If I want to leave, I will. . . .* I'd finished my drink, when I heard my name. He was late, but worth the wait.

Sean was a winner—attractive, with a pleasant smile. The only problem was, there were two of him. I crossed my eyes, and saw four of him. I uncrossed them and still saw two of him.

He looked tense and said, "I don't know how to say this. But, do you remember our phone conversation? I told you I was in Alcoholics Anonymous, and I was looking for a date who doesn't drink alcohol. You said you didn't. Do you remember?"

That was news to me. I would have remembered that question. But I would not have remembered my answer. I might have been looking for sincerity in a man, but I, myself, would have lied my ass off if he sounded like a good dating prospect. My thought would have been, if he's promising enough for a second date, I'll tell him the truth. If one date is all that's going to happen, what the heck.

I tried to look angelic rather than tipsy and said, "I remember the question. I *don't* drink. I'm just tired from work. It was a long afternoon."

"You're sure?" Sean asked, taking the stool next to mine.

I nodded, and he said, "Okay. I believe you. If you say you don't drink, you don't drink. Your word's good with me. I put a premium on sincerity, too."

"Good!" I said, happy that I sounded so cheerful.

Then I passed out and flipped backward off the barstool.

—Brooke, 26, TV cameraperson, Georgia

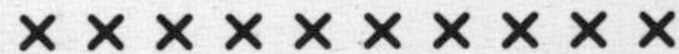

5

Ladies and gentlemen, stop your engines

Going Nowhere Fast

Despite having prepared yourself for every conceivable dilemma, this is still a shocker: a date that's over before it's begun. You primped, you preened, you changed clothes more times than you care to admit. And now you're all dressed up with no place to go.

Keith rings her doorbell and lifts his eyes to the heavens. *Please*, he prays, *don't let this blind date be like the last one. I can't take it again. Let her be decent-looking. Let her read something other than TV listings. Don't let her be the kind of date I want to ask to duck when we pass someone I know on the road. Just this once, and I'll never ask you for anything again.*

His date answers the door, and Keith is happily surprised. She's pretty, is wearing nice clothes, looks interesting, and he smells perfume.

"Hi," he says. "I'm Keith."

She looks him over, waits a few seconds, and says, "What can I do for you?"

He smiles and says, "Marlene? I'm your date. You know, Larry's friend? You work with Larry, and he set us up? I called you Wednesday."

She pauses again and says, "I'm sorry. You must have the wrong address. I'm not Marlene, and I'm not expecting a date. Sorry. Good night."

—Keith, 23, ophthalmology student, Seattle, Washington

× × × × × × × × × × ×

Going to a ball was not an everyday thing for me. I'd never been to one before. I couldn't have created a better date. Boyd was a classic fantasy: tall, dark hair, blue eyes, older—and built.

We'd met at the health club and usually had conversations beside the swimming pool. Monday he told me he was in a jam and needed a date to a ball and wondered if I'd go with him.

I couldn't believe a guy like him would be at a loss for a date but decided it was because, out of all the other women in the kingdom, he pined for me.

I blew a bundle on a long, black, slinky dress that plunged low in back. Then I needed shoes, a bag, a new haircut, new makeup. Dollar signs were popping up at cash registers all over town.

The night of the ball, before I answered the door, I hit myself with some new perfume and checked myself in the mirror for the tenth time. I still didn't recognize myself.

Boyd was wearing jeans, a T-shirt, and loafers. Where was my prince in a tux?

He looked at me and said, "You're kind of dressed up, aren't you? I thought we'd do something casual for dinner, then change into our stuff for the dance. Can you get out of that while I wait?"

That was mood-altering. I felt a little grumpy while I took off my outfit and climbed into jeans.

"You don't mind, do you?" Boyd asked when we were in his car.

The night was gorgeous, and, what the heck, I was flexible. I said I didn't mind. It would be like two dates in one: a regular date for dinner, then a fairy-tale dance.

He pulled into the parking lot of a fast-food fried chicken joint and idled in front of the intercom.

"I'll have the three-piece dinner with mashed potatoes," he yelled into the giant chicken's mouth, then turned to me and said, "What'll you have?"

We ate dinner in a parallel parking space not far away from the intercom. That way, he said, we could get a kick out of how loud people yelled when they placed their orders.

I felt a little better about dinner after we got to the ball. His best friend told me, "You went there for dinner? Huh. I didn't take my date anywhere. I figured there'd be snacks here, and that'd be good enough."

I guess I'd lucked out.

—Lesley, 22, marketing, Trenton, New Jersey

× × × × × × × × × × ×

Keith is skittish as he rings her doorbell and takes a deep breath.

Please, he prays, *at least let this one come outside. I don't care what she looks like. Let her leave her house and get in my car and I'll never ask you for anything that's date-related again.*

Keith didn't enjoy having Marlene, his last blind date, pretend that he had the wrong address. He had gone home and called Marlene, but no one had answered. So he had called Larry, the friend who had arranged the date, and grilled him on Marlene's address. Keith had the correct address, but Larry insisted that Keith must have been on the wrong street. Keith had held his ground, saying he had gone by the house twice. He'd gotten it right.

As recompense, Larry arranged this second blind date, promising Keith that this woman was less picky than Marlene—or the woman Keith thought was Marlene.

Keith's date tonight is Polly.

She opens the door and Keith looks her over, swallows hard, and says, "Ophelia?"

She says, "Pardon me?"

Keith says, "Are you Ophelia? I'm . . . Father Abraham, Ophelia's priest."

—Keith, 23, ophthalmology student, Seattle, Washington

× × × × × × × × × ×

Know how your mind can wander sometimes when you're making love? I kept thinking, *Finally!*

Louis and I worked together, and there was an old-fashioned policy that employees couldn't date each other. This made a little sense, because there were only five of us at our tiny graphic design firm. For five months Louis and I had been looking over the tops of our cubicles, drooling at each other.

He came over that night to discuss a plan. We both realized what a stickler our boss was for maintaining office policies, and—hypothetically, of course—how he'd blow his stack if there was an office romance. We speculated as to how two employees could secretly date.

We could have discussed it at work the next day, so I knew it was just an excuse to come over to my apartment. But it turned out better than I could have imagined, because

Louis and I wound up clenched together, rolling off the sofa and onto the living room floor.

In the middle of things, as I was thinking that Louis and I were finally more than colleagues, I heard a noise in my apartment. I ignored it, but I heard it again and nudged Louis. He stopped moving and listened, too. We both heard the noise. It sounded like a crunch. Louis grabbed a fireplace poker, and we crept around the room. The door to my coat closet was open an inch, and Louis yanked it open. I screamed.

There was a man squatting in the closet, calmly eating a candy bar.

The man said, "You two were really going at it, weren't you? Your boss is gonna kill the both of you, isn't he?"

A burglar had been watching us? My first time with Louis, and we were being scrutinized?

"Better let me go," he said, "and close the front door shut behind me. You're tempting to a crook when all I have to do is give the door a little nudge and then I'm in. Are you two using condoms? You should."

Louis told me to call the police.

While I was dialing—and thinking that Louis and I had to put on clothes if the police were going to come over—the burglar said to Louis, "You can't keep these things secret, you know. You two'll be grinning from ear to ear at work tomorrow, and the cat'll be out of the bag. And you'll be uptight about knowing that I was watching, which is probably a good thing, because you both need a good dose of cold water in your faces if you think you can have sex and work together for a man who's that uptight."

Louis turned to me just a little and said, "If they aren't answering, just call nine one one."

When he turned around, the burglar had run out of the apartment. Louis was still naked and didn't want to chase him.

We never consummated things that night. In fact, we never did. Every time we looked at each other, we remembered the burglar in my closet. Even after I changed apartments and Louis changed jobs, we could joke about that night, but we never did anything about it, because it really was a bucket of cold water in our faces.

—Valerie, 30, graphic artist, St. Louis, Missouri

× × × × × × × × × ×

I make it look as if I just casually happen to drop by Lorraine's office on a Friday afternoon and ask her if she wants to get a drink with me after work.

Lorraine is the big cutup in the state agency in Austin, where we both work. I've wanted to ask her out for months, but it's a joke a minute with her, and I'm not quick on the draw in the wit department. So I tend to clam up around her, which means I haven't asked her out for a date. I haven't had any incentive, either, because she treats me like a pal, which tends to get my goat.

Assuming she says yes, next week it'll be easier to ask her to supper.

She immediately says, "Sure! Why not? Six-thirty okay with you?"

I show up, and Lorraine waves at me from a booth.

I can't take my eyes off her, and I'm about to slide in across from her when I notice there's a guy sitting where I ought to be.

I want to shoot myself and get it over with. He's one of those good-looking types who could do a Chardonnay commercial on TV. Here I thought I was going to be in high cotton, and she brings a date. I'm halfway into my seat already, so I go ahead and plop down.

Lorraine says to me, like it's no big deal, "Dominic, meet

Zach." My brother the investment banker has a dog named Zach.

Even though I want to slam Zach through a wall, conversation starts to move along. But I wish I had Lorraine to myself. Being the third wheel on her date irks me.

At 7:15, Lorraine says, "Gotta go! Going to San Antonio for the weekend. See you Monday, Dom."

She gets up, and I stand to let this turkey out of the booth. Lorraine gives me a peck on the cheek, then gives this jerk the same kiss. He hasn't gotten up.

Then she leaves.

I'm standing beside the booth like a fool, and this guy, who's still seated, says, "Mind if I finish my drink?"

I take Lorraine's seat and say, "You aren't going to San Antonio?"

I'm feeling better already, so I order another drink and already decide that maybe this Zach jerk isn't so bad, after all.

He says he and Lorraine are just friends. We drink and talk for a while, and Zach says, "I'm going to a party at a friend's house tonight. Wanna come? My friend's invited half the town."

Big parties mean babe prospects, and maybe I'll meet someone there to take my mind off Lorraine.

We order dinner and talk about our jobs. Zach's an all-right guy, and it's been a while since I made a new friend. And a new friend who's on a party circuit looks like a pretty good friend to me.

I follow him to the party, and the place is hopping. Good music, good food, and packed wall to wall.

Zach says, "Wanna dance?"

I try not to spit my drink of beer across the room.

Zach says, "You're gay, aren't you? Lorraine said we'd hit it off."

How's that for a great start of a romance with Lorraine? And from Zach's point of view, how's that for the start of a great romance with me?

—Dominic, 38, civil service, Austin, Texas

× × × × × × × × × × ×

I'm late. I'm so late that I wonder if the best thing to do is just not go.

This afternoon I told a friend that I would bail her brother out of a scrape tonight and meet him at his company dinner and party, a black-tie affair. His girlfriend just broke up with him, and he needs a date because he's receiving an award at the party and has to sit with the officers in his company, all of whom either have dates or are married. One of the vice-presidents recommended that this fellow have a date. My friend had set me up on some nice blind dates, so I was happy to do her and her brother a favor.

I had to work late and got home to find that my kitchen was flooded. Then I'd needed a jump to get my car going.

I'm extremely late to this party. Halfway there, I remember that I need tampons, so I pull into a convenience store and buy a box of the bullet-size kind. I cram the box in my little evening bag. I also need gas, but I decide to risk my reserve tank.

My date looks so relieved when he sees me—I'm sure he thought I was going to stand him up.

I skid to a halt in front of him and am out of breath.

He says, "That's okay. Don't apologize. I'm just glad you're here. We've got to hurry. Everyone's already seated."

He takes my elbow, telling me how much he appreciates the favor I'm doing him, and leads me down a small flight of stairs.

I feel myself slipping and lunge for the rail with the same

hand that's holding my purse strap. Grasping the rail, and with the help of my date, I manage not to fall on my derriere, but my purse swings around and around the railing, making a series of smaller and smaller complete circles, spraying the room with super tampons.

—Vivian, 35, nurse, Alaska

× × × × × × × × × ×

Have you ever been in a situation where you're very attracted to your date's friend? Then you know what it's like—sort of exciting and very frustrating.

My girlfriend loved having people around and always invited her friends over for dinner or drinks or to meet us someplace.

She had one friend, Madeline, who was great. My greatest fear, which I guess I suppressed at the time, was that Madeline would go out with one of my friends, so I never invited any of them to my girlfriend's get-togethers. I wanted her off-limits to my male friends. I guess I was trying to save her for myself. Madeline didn't need fixing up, anyway. She always brought a date.

After eight months my girfriend and I broke up. It was more her idea, claiming that she was sick of my always being late. I told her I was happy to escape her manipulative and vindictive streaks. Unlike before, when we'd gotten back together after a few days, this breakup stuck.

A month later I ran into Madeline, and we had drinks. I had forgotten how much I liked hanging out with her. By the second drink, we had both stopped talking about my ex and the breakup, and it was clear that we were extremely attracted to each other. I could finally admit to myself just how gorgeous and sexy Madeline was: red hair, tall, green eyes, great lips, reed-thin.

I called her, and we went out that weekend. I took her to

a party, and my friends were up in arms that I had never introduced them to her. They glued themselves to her, and Madeline was a good sport, flirting and dancing with them, but making it clear she was with me. I lost track of her for a while, because the party was jammed, and when I found her, she was politely refusing to give her number to a so-called buddy of mine.

We went back to her apartment and wound up fooling around, but not going very far. My ex-girlfriend was kind of a specter for both of us.

We went out the next Saturday, and after a few drinks at the restaurant's bar, we couldn't keep our hands off each other. We were seated, and we ordered dinner. After a long kiss, still at the table, I said, "Maybe we should skip dinner." Madeline agreed, and I got up to find the waiter and cancel our order.

At her apartment we didn't waste any time. She took off my shirt, I took off hers. I'd probably been fantasizing about this the first time I met Madeline. She seemed to hesitate a little and grabbed my hand and said, "You know, right?"

I tried to clear my head and said, "Know what?" Then I thought, *Oh, no. Some venereal disease. Well, maybe I can handle that if we take the right precautions. She's worth it.*

Madeline grimaced and said, "Tell me, yes or no. Do you know?"

I sighed and said, "What? You're married? You have crabs? You just got a new boyfriend? You're a felon? I'm shocked. Now I'm over it."

I tried to kiss her again, and she leaned away and said, "I'm a transsexual."

I took my hands off her very quickly.

"You didn't know? Oh, no." Madeline looked upset and said, "I thought you did, but I wanted to be sure, and I wanted to be sure you knew. I've been through some operations, but

I have one more coming up for a sort of nip and tuck. Right now I'm kind of equipped downstairs like you."

Try to maintain a blasé expression when a bomb like that drops. If she hadn't stopped me earlier, I would have found out for myself and certainly wouldn't have liked that.

Madeline said some other things, but I don't remember what, because I was flipped out. I remember reminding myself that I liked Madeline, and that she, or he, deserved more than a look of horror or to have me run screaming out of the apartment. I know that I managed to say, "Thanks for telling me. I'm sure the operation will be a success." The next thing I remember clearly is being in my car and being freaked out, then furious.

The real beauty of this whole situation is that my ex-girlfriend had gotten in her last licks. She knew I'd had an attraction to Madeline, and once she'd teased me by saying she was jealous. My ex-girlfriend was never jealous of any woman. And she definitely knew about Madeline's work-in-progress. She told me every intimate secret that her girlfriends told her—except for this one. My dear old ex had always been into cruel one-upmanship, and when the rumors of this got back to her, she'd have beaten me again.

I still run into Madeline on the street from time to time, and we both stop and talk. I always ask her about my ex, so that I'll know where she is and how she's doing, because I want to know where to find her when I hatch the ultimate revenge.

—Harry, 28, travel agent, Little Rock, Arkansas

× × × × × × × × × ×

We sat on my couch, drinking coffee before we went out to dinner, and for some reason we both wanted to linger over our coffee. My friend Maggie had arranged this blind date. Maggie and I have known each other since we were children.

We had nothing in common other than Maggie, and in a matter of minutes had nothing to say to each other. Our chemistries were repellents to each other.

He was reaching in his wallet to find the address of the restaurant we were going to, and a picture fell out.

I picked it up.

It hit us at the same instant.

"Red MG, and the top on yours was hard to put up," I said, looking at the photo of him, standing beside a car, taken more than twenty years ago.

"Oh, God. It was pouring rain, and you were cranky," he said.

"Was I?" I asked. "I remember that you were bossy."

"Was I?" he asked.

I handed him the photo. He looked very young, posing with his car.

"That was a long time ago," he said. "And that was my first convertible. What a horr—we were on a blind date then, too, weren't we?"

I nodded.

"It was horrible, all right, but I don't remember the details of why," I said. "Should we risk it again?"

I hoped we wouldn't.

"I don't mind saying good night right here, if you don't," he said.

We were both relieved, and impressed, I think, that we had handled this with such courtesy.

And we were also both a little downcast, and I knew why. During the last two decades I had been on so many blind dates that I was at the starting point again, recycling them. And I imagined that he was in the same boat, too. We were both about to start dating our past, and that wasn't something

I was looking forward to. I'd have to slow down on the blind dates.

—Tina, 49, nutritionist, Idaho

× × × × × × × × × ×

Edie was a girl mothers loved and men fantasized about. With her long blond ponytail, she looked innocent and fresh-faced to parents, and like a sexy bombshell to men.

I met her at a washateria. I borrowed her bleach, she borrowed my detergent, and we talked about music for the next hour. She handed me her number on her way out, and I called her from the washateria. She told me to come over.

I drove to her place, and she was in her front yard, at the curb, checking her mailbox.

Maybe she was checking for mail, but if I were Edie, I would have been checking for why it was lying flat on its side.

"My ex-boyfriend ran into it one night," she said, when I asked.

I told her I'd fix it for her tomorrow.

As we got to her porch, I asked her why her screen door was off its hinges, and she said her ex-boyfriend had knocked it off.

She offered me a beer, and I asked her why she had gone to the washateria when she had a washer and dryer right there in her kitchen.

"It's kinda beat up. My ex got mad one night and smashed it with a crowbar."

Well, things happen, and someone this sweet deserved better. I told her I was glad she was out of a relationship with that guy, and she kissed my cheek and said, "You're sweet."

I was standing there in her kitchen, thinking how great a moment that simple could be.

"What's that?" I asked, hearing noise in her backyard.

"Oh, my ex-boyfriend stopped by, and he's chopping some firewood for me. He should come in any second. You'll get to meet him."

What was he doing here? And why was he chopping wood? It was summer.

I put down my beer on her washing machine and walked out the front door and straight to my car.

—Warren, 21, ski instructor, Colorado

× × × × × × × × × × ×

He told me to meet him at the stadium, in front of a certain gate. He was my blind date, arranged for him by his best friend and for me by my best friend. We were going to a football game.

I got to the gate, and there he was, just as he said he'd be, jeans, white button-down shirt, cowboy boots, black rain slicker. He was cute. He handed me my ticket, and I was shocked that it had cost him twenty-five dollars; I hadn't been to a sports event since college.

"Our seats aren't together, because these are the only two I could buy. So I have to go through a different revolving door from you. I'll go through mine, you go through yours, and we'll check out both seating areas and find two seats together."

Easy enough. I watched him go through his metal revolving door as I went through mine, and he vanished. That was the last I ever saw of him.

—Jessica, 26, personal trainer, Dallas, Texas

× × × × × × × × × × ×

His personals ad was heavy on the looks department: "Looking for very beautiful brunette with long hair, slim, tall, preferably green eyes. Blue okay. Nonsmoker. Send photo."

I answered the ad because I felt the same way about men that I met through the personals. They had to be good-looking. I was looking for a man who was tall, blond, and brown-eyed.

I identified with this man's superficiality. One of my friends asked me how I could answer an ad from a man who was so shallow, and I told her it was easy: I'd already gone out with some sensitive what-counts-is-what's-in-the-heart-and-mind types who broke new ground in superficiality. At least the man who wrote this ad was honest.

I could meet average-looking men in person. If I went to the trouble of placing or answering a personals, why shouldn't it be for a great-looking man?

I sent him a photo that looked exactly like me. Nothing staged or retouched. I didn't want to pull any punches. I enclosed a note saying that if he was interested in me, to send me a photo of him, along with his stats.

I received a short letter from him and a photo. He was gorgeous. He wasn't blond, but he was tall, a good weight, had a good job.

He called that night, and we had a promising conversation and set up a date for Saturday.

I answered the door and was taken off-balance. This man was not only nothing like the picture he sent me, he was scary. He looked the way Charles Manson might look if he were able to hold down a steady job. His hair was ill-kept and looked as if he had taken a pair of pinking shears to it. His eyes, instead of being big and confidently friendly, looked beady and colder than a mother-in-law's kiss.

He sat down, then jumped up and paced my living room.

Then he whipped out my photo from his coat pocket and said, "You deceived me. This photo isn't of you."

I looked at the photo and said, "Yes, it is. And it was taken on a day that wasn't going well for me, so it's as close to the real me as a photo's going to get. By the way," I said, taking his photo off my dining table, "who is this picture of?"

He took it from me and said, "It's me, of course. But you tricked me. The woman in this picture is beautiful."

The implication was that the woman in person was not?

"Well," I said, "the man in this picture is Alec Baldwin, and the man in my apartment is a hostile Pee-wee Herman. We're at an impasse."

"This picture doesn't even do me justice," he said, admiring his photo. "I'm told I'm better-looking in person. You know, you could have saved us both a lot of time if you hadn't sent me a bogus photo. There were two other women I could have seen tonight."

"I don't see the point in going out tonight," I said. "Maybe you should take your photo and go."

"I'll leave it here for you, so you'll remember what you missed out on. Where's your phone? I'm going to call another woman."

He took a list of women from his pocket, and I asked to see it. He had already had dates for breakfast and lunch, and there was an *X* beside each name.

"What happened to these two dates?" I asked. "They weren't as good-looking as their pictures, but you were better-looking than yours?"

"Exactly," he said. "Where's your phone?"

Why help him ruin another woman's night?

I told him there was a phone a few blocks away, and that he had to leave.

As I was closing the door behind him, he said, "Try not to deceive men about your looks next time."

Well, how many people are raised to value good looks over personality, a good heart, and honesty? I wasn't. I'd had my fling with superficiality. I never answered an ad like his again.

—Harriet, 47, stockbroker, Florida

× × × × × × × × × ×

Here's how it goes. I meet a girl. We start talking. We exchange numbers, then I call and ask her out. She always accepts. So far so good. Then a day or two before the date, she has an excuse and cancels. Lately they've been canceling the day of the date. So getting through that two-day grace period—if she hasn't canceled within forty-eight hours, the date's on—doesn't hold any water any more. Worse yet, I've developed this theory that women would rather put themselves in danger with someone else than keep a date with me.

I'm a basket case. My therapy group tells me I'm either exaggerating my batting average, or that I'm doing something wrong, or that these women have legitimate excuses, and I'm simply dating high-powered or high-strung women, and not to worry. The group is unanimous in telling me to ask out women who don't seem as if they're overextended.

After two more cancellations in a row, I take their advice.

At the health club, while I'm sitting in the whirlpool, I start talking to this pretty woman—pretty, not a knockout. She tells me she's a secretary. I make a mental note—good job and probably good at it, but not a workaholic. She seems stable and level-headed, not neurotic, as far as I can tell.

On the way out of the club that night, I wait for her. I walk her to her car, and we exchange numbers.

My group is ecstatic the next night. At last I'm gravitating toward a woman they approve of.

I call her, and we make a date for Saturday night. My group applauds. I'm feeling pretty good.

Saturday afternoon the phone rings. It's her. I say, "What's the best exit off the highway to get to your house?"

She says, "This morning I ran into this guy I went to college with, and he's going to take me stunt flying in his plane. It's just platonic. But I can't pass this up. The only problem is, he wasn't that bright in college, and he hasn't flown much, so I hope he doesn't kill me! But it's a chance I've got to take! I'll let you know how it goes! Sorry!"

The most compassionate woman in my group says, "Let me get this straight. This woman canceled you so she could tempt fate?"

I nod and change the subject. The group seems relieved; I've obviously stumped them.

I now have a theory that women would rather put their lives in jeopardy than so much as go to a movie with me. So, optimist that I am, I feel lucky that I can look forward to the chance to know a few stunt doubles, bomb-squad stars, and maybe even a minesweeper.

—Dennis, 26, hotel desk clerk, Nebraska

× × × × × × × × × ×

"Go easy. I think she just got over a semi–nervous breakdown or something."

That's what my friend told me when he set up the date for me.

I'd seen her at a party. She was a Michelle Pfeiffer look-alike, and I was in love.

My friend didn't know the specifics. "Her boyfriend crashed the car with her in it, or she was driving and crashed into him, or the car rolled out of a driveway and hit them both, or the pressure of final exams got to her. I don't know. Now that I think about it, maybe she switched schools just because she wanted to. I don't know. But I heard she's fragile or something. Is your house still a zoo?"

"No," I lied. "We have a maid who comes in once a month, and everyone has gotten really serious about classes, so things are toned down."

There were five of us guys living in a big old house off campus, and we were proud to say that the movie "Animal House" was kid stuff compared to us. Our house had a reputation—not a good one, actually, and it wasn't easy to get women to go out with us, much less come back to the house with us.

There was a sixth roommate—more of a transient, to tell you the truth. He was one of those guys who should have graduated eight years ago, but was still hanging around and coming a little unraveled. He'd stopped paying rent long ago. We let him hang around because we didn't want to deal with kicking him out. Besides, he sort of fit in, in some weird way.

"Three of us are on the dean's list," I lied some more. "Can you get me a date with her or not? Where's she live?"

She lived in the nicest dorm. She was a transfer student, and I was surprised that, during my phone call to her, she accepted a date—she was obviously new to the school. I hoped she didn't tell anyone who knew me that she had a date with me. If she did, she'd probably be advised to break the date.

She was very nervous. We went to hear some music, and even though we danced together a lot, she was still a little skittish. I decided I'd take it slow. Maybe I wouldn't even kiss her good night. Just let her get to know me.

Someone in the dorm had primed her not to go back to my house with me, but I worked on her, telling her I was out of money, and had sodas and beer at my house, that I wouldn't put even one move on her, that she could go home anytime, that I'd leave the front door open, that we'd never leave the kitchen or living room, her choice.

She finally relented. My plan was to let her see that my house wasn't always the zoo it was reported to be—I'd cleaned the place up that afternoon—and that it was possible that I had the makings of a gentleman.

We were sitting on the sofa, drinking sodas—I wanted to make sure her friends knew that we hadn't been drinking booze at my place—and she was loosening up, talking about her classes and her suitemates in the dorm. It was fun.

"You're not as bad as they said you'd be," she said, smiling shyly. "And your house isn't as bad as they said, either. Though I wouldn't live here. . . ."

Excellent! A second date was in the makings!

All of a sudden, she gave a bloodcurdling scream and jumped up, practically coming out of her shoes. She was shaking.

I looked, and I just shook my head, and knew I could kiss a second date good-by.

Wrapped around her ankle was the bony hand of our anorexic roommate, the perpetual dropout student.

He had been under the sofa, probably passed out.

When she stopped screaming, he said one word: "Gimme."

I pried his bony little ghost-white fingers off her ankle, then lifted my hands and gave her a look that I hoped said, "I'm at a loss. Can you believe this?"

She ran for the door.

I sat down and stared at the blank TV screen. So much for a future with her. In the middle of this one date we'd hit the finale.

I felt a bony hand wrap around my ankle, and I realized my roommate was so drunk he was holding on to ankles to keep the room from spinning. I jabbed the remote control, turning on the TV. Just another Saturday night at my very swinging house.

—Craig, 21, student, New Jersey

× × × × × × × × × ×

When I was already fifteen minutes late to pick her up, I had a flat.

If she had been someone I knew, it would have been bad enough, but she was a blind date.

I changed the flat and was trying to make up for lost time when a policeman pulled me over and gave me a speeding ticket. I told him I was late for a blind date, and he worked fast, whipping out a whopper of a ticket in record time and wishing me luck.

Normally I never get flats, and I never speed. And normally I don't go on blind dates. So I'm annoyed with myself and agitated.

I'm a stickler for punctuality, and here I am, over an hour late. I ring her doorbell and roll my head around to loosen up a little, then take a few deep breaths.

She answers the door, and I say, "Hi. I'm Paul. Sorry I'm so late, but—"

My head spins around five, six, seven times? Who knows? Once the birds stopped chirping in my head, and the flashing of a thousand points of light went away, and my eyes uncrossed, and the ringing in my ears faded, I was alone on a dark porch. She had slapped me silly. Someone ought to sign her up.

—Paul, 33, urban planner, Ohio

× × × × × × × × × ×

Here are the two personals ads I narrowed it down to. I was going to answer one of them.

"Easygoing, fun-loving man, 35, loves opera, dogs, rock and roll, jazz, blues, museums, the theatre, fireplaces, seeking warm, loving, giving woman, 25, who can share his fortunes with him."

"SWM [single white male], 34, financial analyst, exceptional income, summer house, nice looking, wants SWF [single white female], 34, with good income, above-average looks. Send photo."

Well, there you have it. Romantic vs. no-nonsense.

The first one had a touchy-feeling quality. The second one was bone-dry eighties business.

I went with Door Number One, the romantic guy. I'm not 25, but I can look 25 if I need to. I'd see how things went, and if the guy was worth it, I'd tell him I'm older than the babysitter he was fantasizing about.

Things could go pretty well. He liked my photo, he said on the phone, and wanted me to meet him for drinks at eight o'clock.

The restaurant hostess smiled a little too chummily and directed me to him.

He looked like a tour guide. Bland features, wearing a navy suit, white shirt, red tie. Looks weren't everything, I reminded myself. Once I got him talking I'd be able to find out if he had anything going for him.

He shook my hand, put on a pair of glasses, opened a folder and said, "Let's get started. You're twenty-five? . . . Where do you work? . . . What's your salary? . . . Where do you live? . . . Do you rent or own? . . . Which health club do you belong to? . . . What are your responsibilities at your job? . . . Where do you see yourself in five years? . . . If you had a management problem involving one industrious employee who alienated all his co-workers, and an average worker who had a way with people, which would you. . . ."

He then asked what business my family was in, and what kind of car I drove.

At 8:25 he closed his folder and said, "That's it! Time's up!"

I felt my eyes get as big as saucers. I'd forgotten that I was on a date, and had actually slipped into my job-interview mode, trying to give the best answers possible, and trying to achieve a manner that said I was as confident as I was creative. It was a few beats before I remembered that he wasn't a prospective employer.

"What do you mean?" I asked, realizing I hadn't even ordered.

"If I'm interested, you'll be hearing from me. Thanks for coming, and good-by." He slipped off his glasses, nodded past me, and sat down again.

Like a robot, I walked out, passing another woman whom the hostess was guiding to his table.

You could tell he was a real animal lover. If I wanted a date with warmth, I should have answered the other one.

—Hannah, 33, dermatologist, Philadelphia, Pennsylvania

6

Take a walk on the wild side

Obsessions and Fetishes

Uh-oh. Stay calm. Act nonchalant. Plaster a smile on your face. You can handle this. These are the dating moments when you have to draw deep on your reserves. You're about to encounter predilections so off-the-wall, sometimes so X-rated, that there's only one word for it all: kinky.

Sweet, modest, Rachel is just the woman to take out dancing with my friends from church. I'm running for an appointment to the church advisory committee, and my previous date embarrassed me with my friends—and hurt my chances—by cursing a lot. Now I'm more cautious.

Rachel and I have been out four other times, and she's great to be around, though a little naive.

She's sitting across from me, and we're at a table with my friends. The evening is going nicely, but I'm keeping an eye on Rachel, since she's drinking more than she usually does. I really don't have to worry, since she's happy to talk recipes with another woman in our group.

I relax and discuss old TV shows with a buddy. "Little Rascals" comes up, and he says he loves the character Alfalfa.

His date leans forward and says, "I love Buckwheat."

I say, "Me, too. But my favorite is Spanky."

Out of the corner of my eye I can see that Rachel is eavesdropping. I guess she loves the show, too.

I continue, "I love Spanky."

Suddenly Rachel jumps to her feet and says, "Spanking! You've been holding out on me!"

—Christopher, 28, image consultant, Pennsylvania

× × × × × × × × × × ×

Victor is uncovering himself to me, one layer at a time. I thought he was kind of a stiff on our first date, keeping our conversations superficial. I decided to give him one more chance, and I'm glad. Tonight, our second date, he's opening up.

I chose this restaurant because I know a lot of the other customers who come here, and I'm friends with two of the waiters. I figured that if Victor was boring, there would be other people to talk to.

I'm not bored tonight. He's confided that he was very upset after his divorce, that he's considering changing fields from insurance to nonprofit work. I decided there's a looser man underneath his gray suit.

Victor says, "I like to take care of women in my life."

"You're a gentleman."

He says, "And I like to bathe women. I could do your toenails for you."

Huh? "I do my own," I say, wondering if he's serious. "I wonder what's taking so long with our order?"

"First I need to be trained and shown how to take care of a woman," he adds, "then I'm her pet."

"You're her *what*?" I ask.

Alec, my friend who's our waiter, comes to our table, gives me a pointed look, and says, "Everything okay, Marcy?"

He's trying to rescue me, and he's trying not to snicker. I should let him help me get out of this gracefully, but I say I'm fine. I've never heard anyone talk like this, and I'm a little intrigued. Besides, I'm in a public place, and I know Alec. If the conversation gets too creepy, I'll just leave.

Victor says, "I've been a love slave for a woman, and I'm looking for a mistress who's a dominatrix." He looks deeply into my eyes and slowly says, "Do you know what a dominatrix is?"

Mr. Rogers gone kinky? I tell him that I know, and I'm not interested.

He says, "You can tell me to do anything you want. I need some discipline in my life."

There's the gong—time to call a cab. I say I have to get up early tomorrow. It's a lame excuse, but it will do. I'm about to say good night, but he interrupts me and says, "Don't leave. I want to take care of you," and drops to his knees beside my chair.

Victor crawls under the table, so that just his derriere is poking out, and grabs my feet, kissing my ankles. He whips off my shoes and starts kissing my toes.

"Stop that!" I say, and whack his derriere with my napkin.

From under the table he loudly says, "Yes! You're embarrassing me! Don't stop!"

Alec appears, and I realize he and everyone else is laughing. I jerk my feet away from Victor and stand up. Alec sticks his head under the table.

Alec says, "Give me the shoes. Give me one. That's good. Now give me the other one. Great."

I put my shoes on while Alec says, "*I* don't want a pet. You need to get out from under there, fella. Let's go."

As I'm leaving, over Alec's coaxing I hear, "I've been bad! Very bad! Tell Marcy I've been . . ."

—Marcy, 37, store owner, Montana

× × × × × × × × × × ×

Dancing would have been the end of me. I'm an aerobics instructor in St. Louis. I'd taught five classes and could barely keep my eyes open at dinner. When he had wanted to go dancing, I almost cried. I said, "How about going to my place and having coffee?"

I was making espressos for us—that would keep me awake, even though it would probably hot-wire him. I thought I liked this guy but wasn't sure. It was our first date, and I was a little out of it at dinner. I wanted to talk to him some more, but first I'd have to wake up to do that. Espresso would help.

I put the coffee and a few cookies on a tray, and walked into the living room.

He was standing in the middle of the room wearing only boxer shorts, socks, and shoes.

I stared at him, he stared at me. There was no passion in the air, nor was there outrage on my part. I was just blown away.

"What *is* this?" I asked, putting down the tray and putting my hands on my hips.

He held his hands out, sort of pleading, and said, "You *said* coffee."

"Yeah," I said. "Coffee. Here it is."

He squinted at me, I squinted back, and then he got

furious and said, "Coffee's a come-on. Everyone knows that. Everyone knows it doesn't really mean to come up and drink some."

He threw on his clothes, acted very indignant, and as he let himself out of my apartment, said, "I don't have time to waste with a prude like you. When you grow up and learn the ropes, give me a call," and he slammed the door.

I was glad I wasn't fully awake for that one.

—Janet, 22, aerobics instructor, St. Louis, Missouri

× × × × × × × × × ×

My youngest daughter took me aside and said, "Mommy, don't go out with him. He's a creepazoid."

But you've got to do what you've got to do. My best friend's husband had set us up.

We got in his car, pulled away from the curb, and he said, "Promise me you'll be yourself. Most of the time, when people are on a blind date, they aren't relaxed. And it's not until the second or third date that they're their real selves, and then they discover what they could have known right away, which is that they don't like each other. For instance, I'll tell you something that I wouldn't have told you until later if I weren't so relaxed right now. I have a lot of really big plantar's warts on my feet. I got them when some new shoes gave me blisters, and things got worse from there. But thank the Lord for laser surgery. Laser surgery will zap them right off. But I have to wait a while before my doctor will do that. Right now they're big, and they're all over the soles of both of my feet. What about you? Have any diseases? Have you ever had warts or anything? I want to know all about you if we're going to be dating. Look in the glove compartment. There're a bunch of brochures for you to look at. Do you see the picture of plantar's warts on the green brochure? That's the one. As long as we don't shower together, I don't think you can catch them. But if you do get them from me, keep in mind that laser surgery . . ."

—Carolyn, 45, librarian, Denver

× × × × × × × × × ×

Only the beginning and the end of the date were peculiar. At the beginning, as soon as Henry picked me up for our dinner date, he said, "You're a songwriter? I've never slept with that kind of fertility before."

What was he talking about? Did he think that because I was in a creative field, I was a wild, insatiable, sexual tigress who was panting to take every blind date around the world a few times?

Somehow, the rest of the date went smoothly. I had decided to pass off his opening remark as nervous jitters. Henry was a little upset by his construction company's recent battles with the economy, and he was a nice, sincere guy.

Afterward, when he drove me home and walked me to my door, Henry was perplexed that I wouldn't ask him inside.

"If you let me stay, I'll do your dishes," he said.

I thought that was kind of cute—I hadn't heard that line before, but I said no. Then I noticed that he had brought his briefcase to the door with him.

Henry tried again.

"When's the last time you vacuumed?" he asked. "Sleep with me, and I'll clean your house."

There was an odd look in his eyes, and the briefcase made me jumpy, so I opened my door, slipped inside, and waved good night.

Henry wedged his foot between the door and the frame as

I was closing it, and I thought he was going to force his way inside.

Instead, he propped his briefcase on his thigh, opened the case, and said, "Look. Look at all this. It's all for you."

Inside was an array of cleaning products.

"Forget the sex," he said earnestly. "Let me do your vacuuming. It's a real turnon for me. Let me do it. You can watch."

—Gail, 31, songwriter, Massachusetts

× × × × × × × × × × ×

Normally I couldn't wait for customers like him just to get out of my way. I was at a convenience store and in line behind a guy who was short fifteen cents. I was in a rush, so I gave the clerk fifteen cents for him, and the customer turned around to thank me. I had just helped out one outrageously good-looking man. After I got checked out, he was waiting for me. He said his name was Brandon—which I think is a very sexy name—and he asked for my number.

He called my dorm the next day and said he wanted to repay me and take me out.

We met for dessert and coffee, which I thought was more original than pizza or a burger. He was witty and superintense, cracking one joke after another. He really got into things, and didn't look as if he was only half listening or half involved in our conversation.

Later, as were walking to our cars, he bent down to the sidewalk and did a headstand. While he was upside down, he said, "I want some Special K."

I laughed.

He stood up, then bent down again, tugging upward at the hems of his jeans, sounding shrill as he said, "Why won't these pants come off?"

"You're trying to take them off over your head," I said, laughing again.

He straightened up, looking past me, and said, "I need Special K. Help me get some."

I laughed and said, "I'd better be going. My car's over there. Where's yours?"

He sat on the curb, pulling at his hair, and said, "Where's my Special K?"

I said, "I have Frosted Flakes in my room. Will that do? I love Special K, too, but I'm out."

"No!" he said. "It has to be Special K."

I pulled a ten-dollar bill out of my pocket, chuckled, and said, "You'll have to buy some."

I didn't expect him to take the money. I was just kidding.

He whipped the money out of my hand and took off on foot.

Another unsolved mystery of a date that seemed to go well but went bad without my knowing it. I called my brother when I got home and cried on his shoulder.

"You thought he was talking about the cereal?" my brother asked. "Oh, brother. Special K is also slang for a hallucinogen, you jerk."

—Sally, 19, student, Richmond, Virginia

× × × × × × × × × ×

I don't think I have ever read aloud from a sex manual. It's weird, and kind of kinky, just like the situation I'm in.

This is my first date with this woman. She lives at home, and after going out for a movie and drinks, we're in her living room. Her parents are asleep upstairs.

She searches through a bookshelf, reaches behind the encyclopedias, and hands me a book, saying it's her favorite.

"It's a sex manual," I say, as surprised as I am pleased.

She finds a dog-eared page, points to the top, and says, "Read this to me."

She sits on a chair, and I stand by the bookshelf, clearing my voice, and looking around the room, waiting for a parent to materialize and slay me.

"Read it," she says again.

I whisper the words, and she starts unbuttoning her blouse. I'm not completely sure what she's doing, because in addition to sneaking peeks at her, I also have to read and watch the staircase. But I do see that her shirt is unbuttoned and that she's staring at me while she moves her tongue across her lips. I'm holding a sex manual—what do I need, a road map? I slam the book closed and start kissing her.

She pushes me away so hard that I start to lose my balance and hop on one leg so I won't fall.

She stands up and loudly says, "What kind of woman do you take me for?" She says this too loudly, because I can hear people stirring upstairs.

"Gotta run," I say, grabbing my jacket and running out the front door.

I get in my car, and I'm fumbling with the key when she runs out, bangs on my window, and says, "I'm sorry if you think I led you on! I didn't mean to give you the wrong idea. Come back inside!"

Her shirt is still unbuttoned. As she presses against the window, the sex manual tucked under her arm, a light goes on in the house upstairs. For one stupid minute I think maybe I will go back inside with her.

Then I throw the car in reverse and hightail it out of there.

—Michael, 25, fireman, West Virginia

I picked him up in the meat department of the grocery store. My line was, "Excuse me. This meat looks okay, but not wonderful. How's yours?"

He was holding a package of steaks and said, "Mine's Choice. Prime."

Yes, I was feeling kind of wild that night.

I told him I was picking up groceries to take to my friends' house for dinner, and why didn't he bring his meat and come with me.

We got in my car, and my friends were surprised when I showed up with this guy. Together, he and I told them how we'd met, and my friends said it was appalling.

He and I were kind of obnoxious, I admit. We were drinking and making out on their couch, and my friends threw us out.

He spent the night with me, and when I woke up the next morning with a killer hangover, he was gone.

Next to the bed were his sneakers, two left-footed sneakers. Stuffed in them were two gloves, two left-handed gloves.

Had he been wearing two left shoes all night? Had he gone home in just his socks? Or had he gone home in two right-footed shoes, wearing two right-handed gloves—and if so, where'd he keep them? I couldn't decode it. It bothered me all day while I was at work.

He called me just as I was heading home, and when I asked how he got my number, he said I'd given it to him. When I asked him his name, he said, "I need my shoes and gloves back."

I asked him why he had left those things, what he had worn out of my house, and why they were all "lefts." I told him it was a puzzle that was driving me nuts.

He said, "Just leave them on your porch. I'll swing by, and pick them up."

I left his shoes and gloves on my porch, with a note that

said, "Please tell me why these are all left-footed and left-handed things." I raced home every day for three days, obsessed with finding out if he had come by and if he had answered my note.

The fourth day I came home, his things were gone. My note was inside the screen door, and on it he had written, "Don't you know?"

Know *what*? I wanted to scream.

That was a year ago, and I still think about it. And my friends still aren't talking to me.

—Josie, 27, textile designer, Philadelphia, Pennsylvania

× × × × × × × × × ×

Believe in high-voltage chemistry. Simply being near him made me break out in a mild sweat.

It was our third date. I'd met him through a video dating service.

We had just returned from a formal dance and were at his house, having a drink. He hadn't made a move, and the anticipation was wrecking me.

Finally he asked if I wanted to see the view from his bedroom balcony, and I played along, knowing that the view was the same ploy as the classic "Would you like to see my etchings?"

He sat on the bed. I sat on the bed. When was he going to make a pass? What were we waiting for? It was up to me.

I was about to kiss him, but he was energetically kicking off his shoes. So I took off my heels.

He took off his socks, and I was confused.

He swayed toward me, and just as I was moving my head into a kiss position, he said, "Do you mind if I pick my toes?"

—Ginger, 34, golf instructor, Tampa, Florida

× × × × × × × × × ×

There was no way I could have lowered my standards any further. If a woman was breathing, I'd go out with her. That was my criterion for a date. Even irregular breathing was fine.

I was in this rut where I couldn't get past the first date with a woman, so that meant I had to go out with new women all the time. Keep those dogies moving.

My friends were getting fed up with my pestering them to get me dates—I'd run through all their friends and acquaintances. If you think they were at the end of their rope with me, you can imagine how I was feeling. But I kept smiling at myself in the mirror, pumping myself up, telling myself to hang in there.

My sister said that the problem was that I am a mayonnaise date. Bland, predictable, comfortable, never new or alarming. I swear that she said "never alarming," but she insists she said "never surprising." There's nothing like a younger sister (an older sister would be more sensitive, I think) to cut through the niceties and lay it on the line.

My sister set me up with Zane. The name made me wince and reconsider my anything-that-breathes criteria. Zane had just started working with my sister at a florist shop.

With my sister's coaching, I designed a Dijon mustard evening. We'd start at an Ethiopian restaurant so we could eat with our hands and sit on little stools definitely uncomfortable enough to be chic. Then we'd go to a semisleazy bar in the East Village so we could pretend that our lives were not in jeopardy as we walked to and from the joint. Nothing boring about buckets of adrenaline shooting through your body. Then, based on what my sister had heard from Zane about Zane's dating habits, we'd wind up at her apartment.

I was willing to do the Ethiopian thing (I prefer a good

diner) and the East Village trip (I'd rather have a beer at my neighborhood Irish pub) if they led to a woman's apartment.

Zane was not at all zany. She was down-to-earth and attractive and a little quiet. With my adrenaline pumping at the thought of the final destination of my plans, I was chattier than usual that night and made up for her silent spells. She kept looking at me intently, probably mesmerized by my range of conversation.

My sister's hipper-than-thou dating itinerary worked. Zane asked me to her place for a nightcap. All I got out of the evening was a light kiss good night, and I wasn't sure the date had gone well, because I *always* thought my dates had gone well until I called for a second date and got the brush-off.

I didn't get the brush-off with Zane. We went out again—I forced my sister to plan that evening, too—and if I had a complaint, it was that she could get quiet and would sort of watch me. But big deal. I got the standard little good-night kiss again. But I could live with it. I was dating again and relieved. I had rediscovered my way with women and trusted my natural instincts that she was a good person to have a relationship with.

Now that I was on the course to establishing the fact that Zane and I were actually dating, after dinner on our third night out, I braved an invitation to my place, and she accepted.

We were making out on my couch, and I was heading to the promised land. Rather, I was trying to get her blouse off. Rather, I was thinking I wanted to get her blouse off. I latched onto the one button on her blouse that was probably glued to a fake buttonhole. I couldn't unfasten it. Granted, I was fumbling. But she wasn't helping, was just watching me intently as always, as if she was trying to figure something out. Then her face cleared, as if a light had gone on in her head.

She jumped to her feet, pointed down at me, and practically

yelled, "You're no Elvis Presley!" then grabbed her purse and left.

The next morning, when my sister called, I told her Zane's parting words. What'd my sister say? "Sure. The last time you got the brush-off was when some woman told you that she actually had a boyfriend who had been torn between her and the seminary and at the last second had chosen her, wasn't it? Why do you always try to save face with me? Stick to the facts. What'd Zane really say?"

—Bobby, 20, mechanical paste-up artist, New York City

× × × × × × × × × ×

"I drove to your house yesterday so I'd know how to get here and wouldn't get lost," he said, standing on my porch. "Let's go!"

We get in his car, and he says, "I had the car washed this morning so it'd be shiny. And I made sure they vacuumed the interior."

He was sweet, going to all this trouble for me, even if it made him sound as if I were the first date he's had in years.

"And I bought a new suit. My secretary helped me find a shirt. My mother helped me with the tie. This morning I got a haircut—I asked one of my clients to recommend a really good place. And I got some new cologne. I called four people about the restaurant tonight. Two people told me Thai food, one person told me Italian, the other told me Chinese. I settled on a Thai place. I called and made the reservations and asked for a table for two near the window but not near a draft. Then I asked my secretary about a bar, and she said . . ."

After dinner, and after a drink at a bar, he's driving me home, ". . . and I thought about our second date and talked to one of my employees, who told me that Middle Eastern was good, so I'll ask around and see if the place he mentioned is good. Then I'll find out if it's casual or formal and if they have live music, which is always a plus. I'd like to find a quicker route to your house from mine, so tomorrow I'll get a map and see if there's a back road to avoid all this traffic. I'm going to get a new shirt and tie so you won't see me in them twice, but I think the same suit will be okay . . ."

—Tracy, 43, hygienist, South Dakota

7

Is that a light at the end of the tunnel—or an oncoming train?

No Way Out

The only thing worse than a date that never gets airborne is the date that you can't seem to escape. You're trapped.

All you need is a way out of this mess, but every getaway route is blocked. Override your panic, think on your feet, and when you see an opening—hit the ground running!

He was irritating, opinionated, loud, and overbearing. And I was at dinner with him. Before we'd even ordered, I was ready to kill the friends who'd set us up. The guy was really out of control—people at the next table were staring. To top it all off, we were at a restaurant that he owned, so no one was going to tell him to put a lid on it.

He was an old-time male chauvinist pig—and every time I argued with him, he'd just smile condescendingly and say something like "You're cute when you're all riled up." When he said that women do their best work in the grocery store or the bedroom, I told him maybe he could keep his waitresses for more than three months if he stopped coming on to them or treating them like slaves. He said, "Can't stick to the subject, can you?" Then he leaned back, smiled, and bellowed, "Just like a woman." That did it.

I threw my napkin on the table and said I was going to the ladies' room. Once inside, I paced around and decided I was not going to subject myself to one more minute with this jackass. But I cringed when I thought about what he might do if I went back out and told him I was going home. He'd turn into a maniac, and I might, too. I thought about racing past his table and making a break for the door, but this guy would probably come running after me. I was trapped.

And then I noticed that one of the stalls had a small window at the top. I went in, locked the door, looped my purse over my head, and put a foot on either side of the toilet seat. Then I reached for the window sill and hoisted myself up.

I poked my head through and looked down. It was a fair-sized drop, a full floor, into an alley. I looked around, trying to see if there was anything I could hold onto to avoid a swan dive. But there wasn't. I pulled my head back in and grabbed an overhead pipe, then walked my feet up the wall and pushed them out the window. As I sat on the window sill, with my feet dangling outside, I heard the ladies' room door open and then quickly shut. I flipped over, jabbing the sill into my stomach. I could do it. I loved the thought of that jerk sitting at the table, waiting for me to come back, humiliated in front of his employees.

I started to slide out, but my shoulders wouldn't go through. I twisted and pushed, finally breaking free. Then I lost my hold on the sill and crashed, my fall broken by a trash can that toppled over and tossed me in some mud.

I stood up and brushed myself off. I was a mess, but I had done it. I heard myself give a very unladylike but very happy snort, and I was glad no one was around to see the mean, satisfied grin I felt break out on my face. I only wished I could be a witness to his expression when I never came out of the bathroom and he stormed into the stall and saw the open window.

Now all that was left was a quick sprint down the alley, and I was out of there.

I looked up and there he was, inside a shadow, leaning on a wall across the alley, calmly smoking a cigarette. The creep had watched the whole thing—and never stopped me.

—Cary, 24, physical therapist, North Carolina

× × × × × × × × × ×

Nothing made me jump more than the sound of a key turning in a lock, especially when I was in someone else's house, and I was in the middle of making love.

She put her fingers to her lips—as if I needed to be told to be quiet.

She threw on her clothes, and I just grabbed mine and my shoes.

I remembered noticing that there wasn't a back door.

I ran to stand flush against a wall that divided her hall from her living room.

I had to take a chance on which way someone would move through the house: probably straight down the hall and into the far part of the living room, or directly into the living room. I put my bet on going straight down the hall and plastered myself against the wall.

The intruder yelled, "Hi, honey! Miss me?"

As he moved down the hall, I moved toward the front door.

Then he said, "How's my wife of one week?"

I hoped his back was to the front door, so I stuck my hand out to slowly turn the doorknob and slip outside, gingerly closing the door.

It had all happened in a matter of seconds: almost being

caught, figuring out how not to get caught, making the escape.

I stood beside her porch, pulling on my clothes, and realizing that my heart was pounding and my hands were shaking. I hadn't known she was married. No wonder she had me park in front of her neighbor's house.

That was more action than I needed. I had heard of articles for married people about ways to add more excitement to their sex life, but I don't think she had read them carefully enough.

—Neil, 34, chiropractor, South Carolina

× × × × × × × × × ×

That was the first and last time I ever wandered far from home on a first date.

He wanted me to take the train from Washington, D.C., where I live, to his house in a neighboring area. I couldn't drive there, because I didn't have a car.

On the train I reassured myself that the date was going to be fun, and that taking risks was worth it once in a while.

Not that he was a big risk. We had met at a museum, both of us admiring the same painting, and had started talking. A guard had asked us if we would leave so the gallery could close. We had a drink together, and he told me that he was a structural engineer. I was a sales rep, and we both had secret desires to paint. The bar had been noisy, but we had had a good conversation.

He met me at the train station, and we were both a little awkward. It had been two months since we'd met, and, for my part, I have to admit that I had worked so hard at reassuring myself that he was worth the trip that in my mind I had made him more attractive and interesting than he was.

At lunch we scraped bottom for conversation. Maybe I remembered a nice conversation that day at the museum because the bar we'd gone to had been so noisy that I couldn't have gotten a good grip on whether we were hitting it off or not. In D.C., everyone talks politics, but he didn't seem to want to.

We ate in silence, then he blurted out that he was handling a touchy work situation by asking a troublesome colleague, "Wanna step outside and settle this?"

I told him that he was inflaming the situation, and he told me that a good right hook always settled work differences.

I wanted to go home, but I had told him I was taking the 6 P.M. train, and it was only 2:00. I didn't want to seem rude, so I decided to make the best of my entrapment and asked him what was next on our agenda.

He told me that he wanted to take me for a ride and show me the scenery.

We were in the car for about three minutes when we pulled into the parking lot of an apartment complex.

"I want to show you my apartment," he said. "I think you'll like it."

More than ever I wanted to get back on the train, but still not wanting to be rude, I followed him inside.

I didn't know what to say. He was telling me that he'd been there for four years, but from what I could see, the apartment looked practically uninhabited.

In the living room were one folding chair and a card table. A TV, stereo, and two large cushions were side by side on the floor.

I poked my head in the bedroom door. On the floor were a mattress and an open suitcase that had clothes neatly folded inside.

"Going for the minimalist look?" I asked, trying to sound light-hearted.

"What? No, not at all. I think it's cluttered," he said.

There was nothing I could see for him to remove. There wasn't even a poster on the wall.

"How about some coffee?" he asked, motioning me to the folding chair.

He made instant coffee in two paper cups and stood beside the card table, telling me another maneuver for handling his problematic co-worker, involving unexpectedly smacking the guy in the face.

"I'd do it like this, pow!" he said, smacking his fist into a hand.

It occurred to me that no one knew where I was. I lived alone and hadn't told anyone I was coming here.

I asked if I could use his bathroom and stood in front of the sink, trying to think. It was hours until my train. What excuse could I come up with for leaving early?

There was nothing in the bathroom except toilet paper. No toothpaste or toothbrush, no shower curtain or soap, nothing in the medicine cabinet. I opened a drawer, and it was half-full of razor blades. The drawer squeaked when I closed it, and I knew he heard, and I was terrified.

I had to go home. He had the car. I didn't know where I was and didn't know which direction the train station was in. Even if I got him to get in the car, how did I know he'd take me to the station? He'd lied about the scenic tour. I had accepted a date with a homicidal maniac.

I opened the door and went into the living room. He had drawn the curtains, was burning incense, and had unbuttoned his shirt.

"I need to go home," I said starchily. "Can you take me to the station now? I need to go home."

I was sure I could have heard a pin drop.

He said, "No problem."

We got in the car, and I was relieved that the door locks weren't electric.

We drove five minutes, then eight minutes, then ten, then I yelled, "Take me to the train station. I told three people your name and that I was coming here to meet you, and if you hurt me, they'll know."

"We're *at* the station," he said, pulling into the entrance, and looking at me as if I were nuts.

I said, "Oh."

—Natalie, 23, gemologist, Washington, D.C.

× × × × × × × × × × ×

I had been over and over this with my father. And he had promised to behave.

I'm on a car date. You know, where your parent drives you to your date's house, then drives you both somewhere. Tonight my dad is driving me and Olivia to and from the movies.

That should be simple enough for a forty-five-year-old man, wouldn't you think? Except that he's a wise guy.

This is my first car date, and for the occasion my father bought himself a stupid hat that he says is his chauffeur's hat, and makes a big deal out of opening the back door for me and Olivia, pretending to close it on me when I try to get in, and saying things like "Did you want to ride in the back with this pretty little thing or up front with me, Master Matthew?"

He's calling me "Master Matthew" a lot, which totally disses me. And he won't tune the radio to anything but an old fogey "easy-listening" station.

On the way to the movies he does all the talking, and Olivia is practically hypnotized and developing a crush on my old man. He's eating it up.

I told him in advance not to pick us up until thirty minutes after the movie was over so that I could have some time with

Olivia, but he's waiting in the lobby of the theater, talking with the popcorn girl.

Now he's asking me if I want him to take the long way or the short way home. "Anything you want, Master Matthew."

Olivia thinks this is funny and is giggling.

Now my dad is saying, "Kind of tough to talk to each other when there's no glass partition between the two seats, isn't it? Too bad this isn't a real limo. Olivia, you're going to have to help Matthew with his homework, and we'll see if his grades can be as good as yours. Doesn't that sound good, Matthew?"

I say, "Dad, could you be quiet and just drive?"

Olivia gives me a cross look, but at least it's a look. She hasn't looked at me since we got in the car.

"Okay," my father says. "Your old dad'll just sit up here alone in the front seat and act as if he doesn't see you. I'm sorry about that. Don't pay me any mind. I forgot my place for a second, and now I remember that I shouldn't have been talking. I'm just the driver and not a real person, even though I get to look at you both through the rearview mirror, so don't even think about fooling around. I'm just supposed to drive. Isn't that what you told me on the way to pick up your pretty date? It's all coming back to me now. . . ."

He talks nonstop, and Olivia is giggling practically nonstop. I'm a caged animal.

When we finally get to Olivia's house, I jump out of the car, and my father opens his door, trying to get out. I glare at him through the window and close his door. Then I run around the car to open Olivia's door, and I hear Olivia giggling some more, and my father saying, "—my pleasure. I hope you enjoyed the movie and—"

I stick my head in the car and say, "Just wait here," cutting him off.

Olivia and I walk to her door, not saying much. I hear my father start the car, and I hope he drives away. I'd rather walk home than get back in the car with him.

I'm in luck. Her parents forgot to put on the porch light, and we're away from my father for a second or two.

We face each other, and I wonder if she'll let me kiss her.

I lean across, and she leans across, and our lips are about two inches apart when my dad blasts us with his high beams.

Olivia giggles and goes inside her house.

I'm going to have to ask Mom to drive the next time. Dad's dating days are behind him.

—Matthew, 15, student, Indiana

× × × × × × × × × ×

I even called him Mr. Perfect to his face, and he didn't seem to mind.

Griffin had to be perfect in every single avenue of his life, not just his work and his clothes, but in his photographic memory of three newspapers every morning, in his meals, his music. He was very successful and as wonderful to be around as he was exasperating.

Griffin was one of the best photographers in New York, and we had met when I was a model for one of his shoots in Florida.

To celebrate our first anniversary of dating, we went back to Florida. Our hotel room was fantastic, and while we lounged around that first night before dinner, he told me that he had been secretly taking sailing lessons, and that he was taking me out at ten the next morning.

Griffin was dressed for our sail in Armani shorts and top, a pair of Top-Siders, and his Rolex watch. I didn't have much room to talk, because I was also in designer clothes, with two-hundred-dollar Persol sunglasses. We looked like two city slicker tourists.

The fellow at the boat rental told Griffin that the Sunfish would be a big enough sailboat for him, but Griffin insisted on a bigger boat. "That small one isn't challenging enough,"

Griffin said to him. To me, Griffin said, "You're going to love this."

Griffin was given a boat with a huge sail, and we climbed aboard.

The day was spectacular, clear and breezy, and we hadn't been out more than five minutes when I could tell Griffin was having a hard time with the sail.

We were a half-hour from shore when the boat tipped and dumped us both in the water. My sunglasses came off and sank, and Griffin's new camera had seen its last, but we righted the boat and climbed back aboard.

I asked Griffin if we should return the boat for a smaller one, and he snapped, "No. This is perfect. I rented a video on sailing and have it memorized. I'll master this in a minute or two."

I was sitting back, having a beer, when the boat dumped us both in the water again. This time we had on our life jackets. I wondered if I should bother getting back in. Griffin climbed aboard, and the boat zipped off. Griffin flew away, yelling for me not to panic.

I had stashed cigarettes in my waterproof camera bag and had been holding the bag when I fell over. I lit a cigarette and lounged in the water, bobbing, while Griffin sailed back to me. There was no way I could get back in. He zoomed past me about fifty feet away, shouting, "Don't go away!"

He zipped past three more times before he got the hang of coming within striking distance of me. I started swimming toward our intersection point, yelling for him to toss out a rope. The wind caught him, and he started to dart off in the opposite direction from me, but I managed to get a hand on the rope. He tried to reel me in, but mostly I got to the side of the boat by pulling myself hand over hand, because he had to spend most of the time steadying the sail. I clung to the side of the boat, with Griffin red-faced and panting. I hoisted myself into it.

Griffin had lost control of the situation and looked freaked out. He didn't know where we were, but we had drifted so far offshore that not only didn't we see land, we didn't know which direction land was in.

Around 3:00 we saw land, and it took an hour for us to maneuver to it. As soon as we could, we dropped the sail and the anchor and dragged ourselves to shore, exhausted from wrestling with the boat.

We were on a deserted little spit of land.

Fifteen minutes later we saw a motorboat in the water and waved to them. The boat drew near, and we yelled to them to go to the boat rental and tell them that we needed rescuing.

We waited two hours, and not only did no one ever come for us, no one was on the horizon.

Griffin got up to explore, in hopes of finding a phone.

"Don't panic," he told me. "I know you're upset, but this'll work out. Are you going to be okay alone while I look around?"

I told him I was safer here alone than on the boat with him, and not to worry about me.

Griffin hadn't been gone more than two minutes when a motorboat appeared and moved directly toward me. The driver waved, cut the engine, then dove in and swam in my direction.

What surfaced was the most incredibly gorgeous man alive—Neptune's son or something.

He was from the rental outfit. No one had alerted him to our situation, but he said he had expected that we'd have trouble and around 5:00 had started looking for us.

He tied the sailboat to his boat, then called to me to swim out. We climbed into his boat. He had a tape deck and some sandwiches, and I was finally having a wonderful time.

Griffin must have been yelling at us for a while before I heard his voice over the background of the water and the radio. I motioned him to swim out, and he did, huffing and puffing when he reached us.

"One of you has to ride in the sailboat," our rescuer said.

I could see Griffin scrutinizing the situation—me happy and smiling, our guide handsome and tan.

"You know more about sails," Griffin said to our rescuer. "You get in the sailboat, and I'll drive this one."

The boat rental fellow said, "Nope. I know the way back. I'll tow you in. Let's go."

I can't imagine that we had to go that slowly, because we were barely moving. I would look back from time to time to see Griffin's face—sometimes furious, sometimes pitiful—while our guide and I cavorted in the motorboat, bouncing to the music and opening beers. The sun was setting, and it was fantastic. I didn't see the point in feeling gloomy. Floating along without my bearings had turned out to be fun for the last hour of a nine-hour excursion.

—Paige, 21, model, New York City

× × × × × × × × × × ×

I'm running down the street, yelling at a taxi to stop.

I just ran out of a man's apartment. It's our second date. The first one had gone fine. He had asked me over tonight to watch a movie. He put a porn movie on his VCR, and when I calmly said I wanted to watch TV instead, he'd gotten upset, then asked me if I ever confused pleasure with pain, and if I'd ever wanted to.

I had grabbed my purse and run out to the street. I didn't even think about staying a second longer. He had run out after me and was only five or six seconds behind me.

The taxi stops, and I fall inside and say, "Go! Hurry!"

As the cabbie pulls away, my date catches up and starts banging on the side of the taxi, yelling, "Stop!"

I'm safe. I wonder if I had panicked, if my date had just been trying to check out my reactions, but on second thought, I actually don't care. The fact that he chased me and now is running after my taxi is proof that I'm doing the right thing.

My cabbie says, "What happened back there?"

I realize the cab is slowing down. I look through the back window and see that my date is still running after us and is gaining on us.

"Just hurry! Speed up! Hurry! Why don't these doors lock? Hurry!"

He slows down some more and says, "I don't know about this. That guy is still chasing us. Did you take something from him or something? I don't like getting messed up in other people's scrapes."

We coast to the end of the block, and my date is close to getting a grip on my door handle.

"Step on it, or I'll report you!" I scream hysterically to the cabbie.

My date has his fingers on the door handle, and just as I think he might yank open the door, the cabbie looks in the side-view mirror and says, "Oo. What a creepy-looking guy," and jams down on the gas pedal.

—Teresa, 38, court reporter, Illinois

× × × × × × × × × × ×

When I woke up, the bedroom was full of candles, and there was a big picture of James Dean propped up on her bureau, with a bunch of candles around it. She was standing in front of it, naked, sort of chanting.

Well, it's not that she was Princess Di and was keeping a secret from Charlie. I had just met the woman at a bar and gone home with her.

When I got there, the poster hadn't been out, and she'd only lit one candle.

She looked at me and said, "He talks to me at two A.M. Tonight he said that I should marry you."

She sounded kind of sweet.

She added, "I looked in your wallet and found your job I.D. card, so now I know where you work. And I wrote down your address and phone number. I kept one of the deposit slips you had in there, so now I know where to set up our joint account. Tomorrow you should bring your things over and move in, or I'll have to go to your office and talk to you about it."

Uh-oh. My dating luck had taken a nosedive. I had rolled snake eyes tonight. It was bound to happen sometime.

I told her sure, sure. I'd be sure to do that tomorrow, but tonight I had to go home, because Jimmy Dean told me I should.

She cleared up fast and said, "Don't give me that bull. He can't talk to you or me. Now get back in bed."

I went to the front door, but she blocked it and wouldn't let me out.

I went to the back door and remembered that we were under a tornado alert. It was windy and pouring sheets of rain. But being outside was safer than being in with her.

"You'll never get out of the complex," she said. "The security here is the best."

Well, there was a time when every man faced a test of wit and brawn.

I went out the back and got pelted by rain. I was trapped on a little deck that was hemmed in by a seven-foot wood fence.

She had a flower trellis against it, so I climbed it and went over the wall.

I still wasn't getting anywhere. Now I was in a communal courtyard that had a tall concrete wall around it.

I stacked two flower barrels against the wall so I could step up onto them and hoist myself over.

Lights were going on in some of the town houses, and I kept running, telling myself that it was like being at Stalag 13, and that I was Hogan, leading the Heroes to safety.

I still wasn't through. There was a metal fence that sealed off the whole complex from the street, and the gate only unlocked with a code.

I was in trouble. If they caught me, they'd book me for something. No one would ever believe that I went through all this because I got spooked by a bad date.

I climbed a tree, ripping the crotch of my pants, and fell the ten feet to the ground on the other side.

I took off again, limping this time, and got into my car.

I didn't put on my lights, just hunted for the exit out of the parking lot. You needed a security card to lift the wooden arm that blocked the exit, so I swung my wheel to the right, gunned the engine, and popped the curb, bobbing onto the street.

In my rearview mirror I could see the little security car, like a tiny golf cart, trying to come after me, and getting smaller with every second. I'd made it.

Except, I was low on gas. I patted my pants pocket and realized that my wallet was gone. She probably had it. I didn't even consider going back, because I wasn't sure that I could get out again.

—Fred, 28, musician, North Carolina

× × × × × × × × × ×

Elliot tells me his house is about forty-five minutes from town, in an undeveloped area. We're on our third date, and as he pays for dinner, he asks if I want to see his house. I know this is an invitation to sleep with him, and I say I'd love to see his place. It seems appropriate, I think to myself, that he would live that far from town. I met him at the health club before work one morning, and he's a strong, athletic man, very confident, without being a macho pig.

It's a nice night, and the drive is pleasant. At his house Elliot takes my coat and asks if I'd like a drink. We smile at each other, and I nod. The doorbell rings. Elliot's face goes ashen, and he says, "Hide. Get under my bed."

I say I certainly will not, but he says, "Please. I'm begging you. Just for five minutes."

He looks terrified, so I say, "Okay, okay. But tell me why."

"No time," he says. "My bedroom is that way. Hurry."

I sit on the floor between his bed and a wall and try to hear what's going on in the front part of the house, but I can't make anything out.

The conversation is slowly coming my way, and I can tell Elliot is with a woman. Then I hear, "I know damn well there's a woman in this house, and I won't leave until I find her and tear her hair out."

Uh-oh. That would be me. That would be my hair she wants to tear out.

Elliot doesn't sound equipped to handle her. She sounds tough and mad, and he sounds scared and unconvincing.

"There's no one here. Really. Believe me. How about a drink?"

"When I get my hands on her, I'm going to kill her," the woman says again.

They're only one room away, and I notice a window next to me. I wonder if I'm overdramatizing the situation, but I open it and climb out. Just as I'm clear of the sill, Elliot and the woman enter. She is a big, square block of a woman.

Elliot looks as if he might have a coronary, and she notices.

"She's in here, isn't she? Time to come out of hiding, you little bitch."

I'm transfixed at the window, watching her whip open the closet. She drops to the floor, and Elliot says, "No! Get up!"

She gives him a glare that makes my skin crawl and looks under the bed.

Elliot looks as surprised as she does when she says, "No one under there."

I could kill Elliot when he says, "Are you sure?" and looks under the bed. He puts his head up and says, "Just kidding. Satisfied? Can I show you out now? We're not dating any more, remember? You're not supposed to come by any more, remember?"

She looks at the window I've crawled out of and says, "You never open that window. Looks like someone made a little escape, and it's pretty cold out there, so good luck."

I glue myself to the side of the house and hear her slam the window and lock it.

Whoever she is, she's right about one thing. It's cold out here.

My purse and jacket are inside, but I know that I had put money in my pocket. I dig into a pants pocket and find ten dollars. I tell myself, I can do this. I can handle this as long as I don't panic.

I go to the road and start walking. After a half-hour, I hitchhike a ride to the nearest gas station. I'll call my roommate, and she'll come get me.

I thank the driver and get out of the car. He leaves, and I realize that the gas station is closed. That's okay. I don't need to be inside. There's a pay phone.

First, I'll call Elliot.

"Hi, I'm at the gas station. Help me!"

Elliot says, "What number are you calling?" then hangs up.

I'm stunned. I dial again, and he says, "You have the wrong number," and slams down the receiver.

This is great. My wonderful, manly date won't even have a phone conversation with me and doesn't care what's happening to me or where I am.

That was my last quarter. I call collect to my apartment, but my roommate doesn't answer. Then I remember that she said she might go away for the weekend. I feel like becoming a vegetable and would like to do anything other than think, because I don't know what to do next. How am I going to get home?

I'm freezing, so I decide to hitchhike back to Elliot's house.

A teenager picks me up but says she won't let me use her parents' phone to call a friend from work, and doesn't go for the idea of my standing in her parents' yard while she makes the call for me.

"No way. My parents'll ground me for picking up a hitchhiker. I should never have stopped."

She drops me off a block from Elliot's house; I don't want anyone to see me. That woman scares me, mostly because Elliot seems helpless with her.

I'm in front of his house, but big deal. Her car is still parked out front. I can't ring his doorbell. I creep around his house to the bedroom window, thinking I'll crawl back in, but he's in bed with her.

Frankly, I'm relieved that I'm not the one in bed with him.

I open the garage door and brace myself to get caught, but no one comes to check. I shut the door, find a bunch of paper grocery bags to use as a blanket, and climb into the back seat of Elliot's car.

The next morning, hearing car doors close, I wake up. I hear a car drive off. I realize where I am and why I'm in a garage, and I'm furious at Elliot and at myself.

I get out of the car and bang on his back door until he opens it. He actually looks irritated that I'm here.

"Thanks for your help last night," I say. "I don't know what I'm happier about, having to hide or freeze outside or having you pretend it's a wrong number. You're terrific. Just give me my things, and let me call a cab."

"Cabs won't come out here," he tells me, still not letting me inside.

"Then get dressed," I say, pushing my way inside. "You're driving me home."

"Now?" he asks. "I had a heck of a night. Do you mind if I take a nap first?"

—Yvette, 37, social worker, Michigan

× × × × × × × × × ×

One more glance at my watch, and I'm out of here. I've been waiting almost an hour for a friend to show up.

I catch the eye of a cute guy two barstools away, and he sends me a drink. I send one back to him, and he scoots over to an empty stool near me and introduces himself as John.

John's in town on business and was supposed to meet some of his colleagues here, but they're not showing up, either.

He tells me that his company is having a party at the hotel they're all staying at and asks if I want to join him.

This is the kind of overture that I usually brush off, but he seems like a genuine guy, and I don't think he cooked up a story about colleagues and a work party. I don't feel like going home, so I take him up on his offer.

As we walk into the lobby of the hotel, I expect him to say that he can't remember where the party is, and why don't we go to his room. But John takes me directly to an elevator, and when we get out, we walk into a small conference room, where there definitely is a party in progress. It's nothing exciting, lots of conversations about work, but it's not too bad. My date is considerate, introducing me to everyone, whispering occasional private cracks to me that, I have to admit, are pointedly funny.

Around midnight the party thins, and John moves me to a

corner of the room. I prepare myself for "Would you like to come up to my room?" That will ruin everything.

He starts in on this line, saying, "I wouldn't normally ask you this. I hope you aren't offended. But I'm really jet-lagged, and I need to go to bed. Can I get your number, and we'll get together tomorrow? I'm here for a week."

I'm secretly relieved; maybe there's a future with this date, after all. We exchange numbers, and John takes me to the elevator. He says he'll walk me to my car, but I tell him not to bother, that I'm parked near the front door.

Our quick kiss good night turns into a long, wonderful kiss, and I step into the elevator, feeling light-headed.

I float across the elevator lobby, laughing to myself that all night long I had expected the worst from him, and he had turned out to be a perfect gentleman.

I'm almost in the revolving door when two security guards step in front of me, and one says, "Come with us."

I refuse, and they tell the front desk to call the manager.

I follow the manager to his office, giving him grief about the security guards.

The manager holds up a hand and says, "This hotel is cracking down on hookers. Hope you have your bail lined up."

Is he talking to me?

One of the guards says, "A guest in the hotel reported seeing you groping a male guest in front of the elevator."

"We weren't groping," I say, feeling as if I'm in a bad dream. "We were kissing. And I'm not a hooker."

I'm wearing a black miniskirt, fishnet hose, black suede over-the-knee boots, a turtleneck sweater, and a peace symbol on a leather string. I'm in a sixties outfit, the latest thing for the nineties, and these bozos think I'm a hooker? What an insult.

I explain this fashion trend to the manager and start pulling out I.D.'s and business cards pertaining to the catering business I'm part of, telling him about the party I had just come from.

He looks a little unsure of himself, and says, "What's the name of the guest in the hotel?"

Great! I'm going to be off the hook. John. Now, what's his last name? I can't remember, but that's not a problem, because he wrote it down. I fumble through my purse, looking for the piece of paper but can't find it.

The manager and guards are looking at me as skeptically as I'd looked at John when he said "I don't normally do this kind of thing."

"I know!" I say. "If I take you to the party room, will you believe me?"

The manager says his records didn't show a party, but that if I show him the room, he'll let me go.

The manager, a guard, and I are on the elevator, and I'm sweating bullets. We get off on the fifth floor, and I know I'm off the hook, because I remember exactly where it is. I turn the handle, and it's locked. The manager unlocks it, and it's empty, except for the sofa and some chairs, no evidence of a party. Maybe it's the wrong room.

The manager takes me to three more conference rooms in the hotel, and they're all empty. He and the guard give me this "Now do you give up?" look, and I follow them back into the elevator.

As we get off the elevator and walk through the lobby to the office, I know I am up a creek. No one believes me, and I'm at a loss for how to convince them.

If it looks like a duck, and quacks like a duck, what is it?

So I stop in the middle of the lobby and loudly say, "I am a respectable businesswoman with a catering business. And if you call the police, and if I am booked, I will sue the living daylights out of you and this hotel, and make the front-page news in this town and all over the country for harassing women, got that?"

The manager sighs, flicks his head to the guard, and they leave. I would like an apology but decide not to pursue it.

Driving home, while I'm still shaking and angry, two other thoughts come to mind. All night I'd been misreading my out-of-town friend, and my comeuppance was that I would be misread by a hotel manager. If I had thrown caution to the winds and wound up sleeping with John, I wouldn't have been nabbed in the lobby. There is a sort of dating justice in the world, and it is skewed every time.

—Audrey, 27, caterer, Delaware

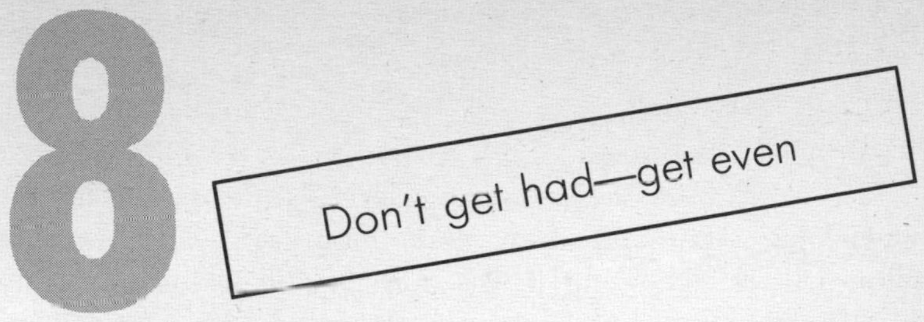

Revenge

Surviving a rock-bottom date was torture, but worth it for this moment: You're about to get the last laugh. You've dreamed about settling the score, but in the past, you've been too paralyzed with surprise to respond when you've been treated badly. Not this time!

Sometimes the revenge you choose is subtle and clever, other times you get carried away . . . but it's always sweet.

"Love Scrabble, mystery movies, and Sunday mornings in bed with mimosas and crossword puzzles."

That line in his personals ad grabbed me, so I wrote him. Ken called and we had a wonderful conversation. He was with a management firm, and his role was to travel across the country giving lectures on motivational training. Since I'm in personnel, we could swap work anecdotes. I was happy he suggested a Thursday night date. He gave me a number to call to confirm our plans.

Thursday I called the number to say I was still on for that evening, and the voice sounded familiar.

"Susan?" I asked.

"Bridget?" she asked.

Ken used the same answering service I'd been using for seven years. And in all seven years, Susan had been answering phones there. I thought it was odd that he hadn't given me his office number, but I left my message.

For the next three months, Ken and I went out once or twice a week. Because of the demands of his job, his hours were erratic and he traveled constantly, so we had dates at unusual hours. For instance, he might stay over on a Friday night but on Wednesday would meet me for dinner and leave by ten. We only had one Sunday morning like the one he'd described in his ad.

Ken said he should have let go of his answering service long ago, but it was an old habit that he hadn't gotten around to giving up. Considering the amount of time he was on the road, he said, the service made sure that personal calls didn't get lost in the shuffle of business calls. He told me his office phone was primarily the portable cellular he carried in his briefcase.

Going into our fourth month, two days after we said the "I love you's," I left a message with Susan at his service. My message said, "Did you forget we had a date last night? I should have told you it was my birthday."

Instead of saying "Okay! Got it," Susan was quiet, then said, "How many times a week do you see him?" After I told her, she asked, "What times does he meet up with you?"

I was taken aback and wasn't sure I wanted to have hit such a jackpot. Susan was in a position to know everything about Ken's personal life. Clearly there was something she wanted me to know, but I knew she could get sued for telling me, so I played along, answering her cryptic questions.

Finally she said, "Things are not what they seem." She repeated this, sounding like a character in "Twin Peaks," and when I pressed her to be specific, she got off the phone.

True, I had never been to Ken's office, but he had never been to mine, either. We worked on opposite ends of the city. And true, I'd only been to his apartment a few times, but so what? His place was kind of bare and antiseptic; he was a classic bachelor who didn't seem to know how to decorate.

He stood me up a month later, and this time, when I left a "What happened?" message with his service, Susan said, "Bridget, haven't you figured it out? Does 'mystery movies and crossword puzzles' sound familiar? Look in the paper this week. He's dating about fifty of you at the same time, using that ad. He's constantly answering personals and writing them for papers up and down the West Coast. He has time slots for these dates. I wish I could show you the stack of messages for him. I don't know how he keeps it all straight. No wonder he slips up sometimes."

And no wonder he loved mystery movies—he was starring in his own.

When I confronted Ken, never mentioning Susan, only saying that I suspected he was still running ads and going out with women who wrote him, he was upset. His explanation made sense. He had placed ads in several papers, and some had been scheduled to run months after each other, and so, sure, people were writing him, but he wasn't responding.

I decided that though Susan had been trustworthy and efficient for years, she was misinterpreting his messages. He had probably run his number in some of the ads.

I was at the sixth-month mark in our relationship when an out-of-town girlfriend called to say hello. We hadn't talked in a long time, and she filled me in on her personal life by raving about a man she'd met three months ago when she answered a personals ad in her local newspaper. She was in love and said he was, too. The ad had been about "Scrabble, mystery movies, and mimosas." That's all I needed to hear, but I asked for his name, anyway. It was Ken.

Stunned, I filled in my friend—that way we could both be

stunned, I guess. The pieces came together. We decided his place must be a company apartment. Then I told her about Susan and that I had to call her.

"You warned me," I told Susan.

"Here's something neither of us knew till today," Susan said. "I think he's married. A woman who answered his ad a few months ago called today and thought I wouldn't recognize her voice. She tried to sound casual and asked if I had his wife's number—she claimed she and his wife were friends, and she'd lost his home number. What do you think? Is he married, or is this woman just fishing around to see if he's married?"

I wondered. I hung up, listened to Ken's voice as he left a message on my answering machine, then picked up the phone and dialed our mutual service.

Susan answered, and I persuaded her to tell Ken, the next time he checked in, that his wife had called and was responding to his love of game playing and mysteries, and to please call when he had a spare moment between ads.

Susan said, "Okay. I'll be sure he gets the message. Good night."

I barely slept that night. I couldn't wait until noon, when Susan said Ken always called in for messages. At noon I called Susan.

Yes, he'd called. Yes, she'd given him all his messages, and he'd been flabbergasted, spilling out, "My wife called? Are you sure? Are you positive?"

I checked in with Susan twice a day for the rest of the week. He called his service three times a day for his messages, always asking, "Any other messages? Are you sure you gave me all of them?"

She said his messages were slowing down. Obviously *he* was slowing down, not responding to fresh ads. Women were calling back, leaving messages that they were upset that he hadn't returned their calls. Ken was groaning when Susan would list the women who had called for him. Every day he asked Susan, "Any messages from my wife?" Once he asked, "You'd recognize my wife's voice if she called again, wouldn't you?" Susan said no.

Two weeks after the phony call, Ken gave me a hangdog look and told me that he was being relocated. I played along, acting upset, and said I'd move with him. If he was too proud to ask me to move, I'd find him one way or another, and he'd come home one day and find me waiting.

He looked dumbfounded, said he had to go, and would call later. I never heard from him again.

But I did hear from Susan. Four months later, as the calls for him died down to hate calls from women whom he had left, he canceled his service. After he thanked Susan for her help over the years, his final words to her were "No other messages today? None? Not even from my wife?"

I still scour the personals sections, because I still answer some. And I still hunt for his type of ad, but it's been a year, and I haven't seen a mimosa in any of them.

—Bridget, 35, personnel, California

× × × × × × × × × ×

I've had some wildly unsuccessful dates. I feel as if I specialize in them. There was the woman who turned the date into a "Jeopardy" spelling quiz. "How do you spell *unconscionable*? How do you spell *hors d'oeuvre*?" Then there was the one who told me everything I liked—crossword puzzles, Nintendo, bridge, poker—was juvenile.

That's the one I dated for five months, putting up with these put-downs and hoping for the best. Her name was Rhonda, and I was still hoping for the best when she dumped me the night after I took her to my parents' house for Easter dinner. It took me a couple of months to recover from that bomb.

That's why I stayed calm when Rhonda called in June. I'd known she would. For someone as lofty as she was, she couldn't figure out her computer to save her life and was too embarrassed to ask for help more than five times a day from her colleagues at the department store.

Rhonda said she was at her office and was having trouble with the new accounting system they were using, and was making a mess of her day's work. I design software and knew this system inside out.

I told her to send a copy of her working disk to my office, but instead, she wanted me to go there around 7:00.

When I arrived, I was cool, even though Rhonda acted as if we were great friends.

I retrieved information she thought she had lost, straightened up what she needed, and gave her a minilesson. Then I did what I'd been dreaming of doing.

I inserted a line into the system that would pop onto her screen and onto every other screen at the store every time she logged onto her terminal. The line said, "Rhonda is always promoted over her head and needs outside assistance with her job."

"All done?" Rhonda asked, hanging up the phone and putting on her coat. "That was my boyfriend. You'd love him. I can't wait to introduce you. He told me to tell you that there's a woman at his office that he thinks you'd be right for. Maybe we can all four go out sometime."

Really? I hadn't even met the guy she dumped me for, and the two of them were playing Santa Claus for me?

I smiled and said, "Yup. You're all set. Is your boss still giving you grief about your screw-ups at work?"

"Yeah," she said, putting on lipstick. "But I keep bombarding him with work I'm doing great on and hiding the stuff I don't understand. He thinks I'm over the hump. Let's go."

We were outside her building, and Rhonda waved and walked to her car.

I had second thoughts about what I'd done to her computer, but the building guard wouldn't let me back in to fix it. As I drove off, I remembered the flip statement that Rhonda had given me when she called to tell me she didn't want to see me any more. "You'll get over it," she'd said. Well, now we'd get to see if there was something *she'd* get over, and I didn't feel so guilty any more. In fact, I would call her the next day, to have her tell her boyfriend to set me up on that blind date.

—Harley, 27, software designer, Minnesota

× × × × × × × × × × ×

After five months of practically being inseparable, he stopped calling, wouldn't return the calls I left on his answering machine at home, had coached his doorman to tell me he wasn't there, and instructed his secretary to screen my calls and show me to the door when I went by his office. It was a complete disappearing act.

For a week I tried to get in touch with him. I didn't know what had gone wrong. At first I left furious messages and notes, and then I was embarrassed about revealing how crushed I was. I was close to coming to terms with the fact that we were through, but I wanted to make a point in a way that would throw him off-balance.

A mutual friend told me that he was making a major presentation at 11:00 on Friday morning, so I arranged for a costume to be sent to his office then. It was a Houdini outfit, complete with handcuffs and a straightjacket. The card I had written said, "Next time dress the part."

I hear that although there were some chuckles at the meeting, it wasn't a totally light-hearted reaction.

I found out that he had dumped me so completely for his boss's daughter. His boss was the second person in that meeting to read the card, and his boss is a woman. Rumor had it that she didn't laugh.

—Gwyn, 29, ice cream distributor, Tennessee

× × × × × × × × × × ×

Women spurned are dangerous. I know this is true, because this particular woman had the capacity to smash my windshield or mail me a dead animal.

It was Cynthia's idea to "stay friends" by going out one last time. I had dumped her, so I thought this was bonkers, but I went along with it, anyway, because she had a real edge to her.

Creepy enough, she chose the club we always went to, on the outskirts of town.

Cynthia was acting so sweet and loving that I couldn't figure out why we had broken up. Where were the usual rages about my making whistling noises when I tried to get food from between my teeth? Instead of barking a drink order to me, she politely asked, "Would you mind getting me another drink?"

I was at the bar, waiting for her drink while I sipped my beer, when I got a mean poke in my back. I turned around and was surrounded by four of the biggest guys I had ever seen. Monstrous. In-bred, maybe. They were expanded, pumped-up guys—they reminded me a lot of Hans and Frans, from "Saturday Night Live." One of them—the biggest one, "Frans"—sneered. "You Owen?"

I said I was.

"See her?" he asked and pointed across the smoky little joint. At the end of his finger, smiling and waving—and standing with her arm around the bouncer—was Cynthia.

"That's our cousin," the guy said. "And we don't like it much when someone proposes marriage, then dumps her. Know what we do to someone who does that?"

I had never discussed marriage with Cynthia, but that wasn't the issue. I wondered how much damage they wanted to do to me.

"We take him out back, and the four of us kick his ass and smash his face until he won't be pulling that routine on anyone else. You get me?"

It looked bad. I was going to be turned into a doormat. Even if I could have gotten past that goon squad, Cynthia had the door barricaded.

I said, "Well, if you're going to kick my ass, there's nothing I can do about it. But before you do, do you mind if I finish my beer? It'll be the last cold one I'll be able to drink for a while after you get through with me."

They huddled, and the big one said, "Okay. But make it fast."

The bartender said, "You gonna pay for these or not?" He'd lined up four beers beside Cynthia's drink, trying to jack up my check.

I said, "I didn't order these," and the bartender said, "Bullshit." I had enough trouble, so I paid for them.

I told "Frans" and his friends, "I paid for them. Help yourselves. Then let's go let you kick my ass."

Without having to huddle, they grabbed the beers, and we stood around silently, looking at the crowd, listening to the band warm up after their break.

One of them actually lowered his beer and asked, "Why'd you do that to Cynthia?"

"She's got her version of what happened, and I've got mine," I said. "She's entitled to hers. It doesn't matter. I understand that whole family honor thing. You've got to do it."

I was buying for time, hoping some solution would come to mind. No solution was coming to mind.

After a minute another one said, "You picked the wrong place to be at, and tonight you find out why. Let's go."

Well, we went to two other clubs that night, and they were

right: The music was better at those places than at my usual hangout.

They never did kick my ass. They had shoved me in the car, driven around, then paid my cover charge each time. I always bought a couple of rounds. We never talked about why they had had a change of mind, and I never asked—I didn't want them to reconsider once they thought about it.

They dropped me off at my car around 3:00 in the morning and Frans said, "Let's do it again sometime." I shook hands all around.

I knew Cynthia was waiting up for them, and that she'd be spitting bullets when she found out that we'd gone partying. I spent the night at my brother's house and made sure all the doors were locked. I checked twice.

—Owen, 21, horse trainer, Virginia

× × × × × × × × × × ×

This business trip is turning out to be fun, unlike the other trips that haven't been panning out lately. I'm an investment banker, and I just set up the framework for a deal, so I'm celebrating by having a drink at the hotel bar.

It may be thirty degrees in Boston, but here in Mississippi, it's sixty-five. The weather feels great, and I feel great. Fridays like this are tough to beat.

I guess I'm staring at this gorgeous blond a few chairs down from me, because she blushes. I wave, she waves back, and I stand up and go over to her. We introduce ourselves, and she tells me she works at a local TV station. I make a mental guess that she's about twenty-eight. She's going dancing with the friends from work she's with and invites me.

I don't have to be back in Boston until Monday afternoon, so instead of leaving Saturday morning, I stay in Mississippi, spending the weekend with her.

We're great together. We like the same kinds of food and music, and we're simpatico in bed. She's got a quick wit, and a lot of our conversation is about one-upping each other with funny remarks, so even talking to her is a turnon. The best part is, she's sweet and smart and says she likes me.

At dawn on Monday morning I tell her good-by and race to my hotel room to check out. On the plane home I'm feeling kind of sad. I wish she lived in Boston.

I call her that night, and we talk on the phone for an hour.

I invite her to come to see me in Boston, and three weeks later, she's in my bed, and we have another great weekend together. There's no one in Boston I like this much.

After she goes home, we talk on the phone a lot—three or four times in one week. Then two times the next week. Then one time the next week. By the end of the month, she's leaving messages at my office and home that I'm not answering. It's not that I've met someone new, but, I just think, since we don't live in the same town, what's the point? I'll let this wind down and blow away.

I get home, and there's a package from Mississippi on my doorstep. I'm excited. A present! And it's guaranteed not to be cookies from Mom—my usual "gifts." It's from my Mississippi babe. Maybe I should call her; I haven't returned any of her calls in two weeks.

I race inside and tear the brown paper off the package. A shoebox? Well, she has great taste, so they've got to be good shoes.

A pair of shoes it ain't. A voodoo doll it is. Of me. And I've got to hand it to her, it isn't a cheesy knock-off of a voodoo doll. It's authentic. It's so authentic I feel as if I'm in a bad movie. My skin crawls. If there were a camera over my shoulder, I could be a bit player who's about to meet an untimely fate in the movie *Angel Heart*.

It has *X*'s for eyes, red hair like mine, and it's stuffed with straw. Here's the worst part. It's covered—every square inch of it—with pins. Every inch. Including the important part—the genital area, *my* genital area. It's painful just looking at it.

I remove the pins from the genital area and then decide not to remove the other pins. For a second I think I ought to do what a friend of mine would do: bite the head off this doll and mail it back to her, just to let her know I'm not intimidated. But I'm not him. That would gross me out. And, I figure, this doll is the ultimate touché.

I deserve it. She's a smart, hip woman, and this is an original "take that." It speaks volumes—to *me*, anyway.

So I prop up the voodoo doll on my TV set.

It's an interesting conversation piece, definitely an accessory you don't find in a furniture catalog, and definitely more fascinating than a picture of myself. No one can accuse me of vanity.

I've never called her. What would I say—I got your message?

It's been six months since I got the voodoo replica of me in the mail. Maybe it's a coincidence, but that weekend in Boston, when she visited me from Mississippi, was the last good date I've had. I've also been wondering why my mattress feels as if I'm sleeping on rocks, and why my body has some weird aches these days . . . Naa . . .

—Reed, 35, investment banker, Boston, Massachusetts

× × × × × × × × × ×

Never accept a date with someone you meet at a costume party. I was dressed as Marilyn Monroe. Ed came as the Lone Ranger. Not only was he wearing a mask at the time, but his costume turned out to be more tasteful than his everyday clothes.

He said he was in real estate. For our date, he took me to dinner at a steak house where he's a regular, and as he shmoozed with the maître d', I caught a look at myself in a mirror, and I was squinting. His beige summer suit was too tight, à la *Saturday Night Fever*, and the diamond stud in his ear was too big.

We were shown to a table, and he ordered a porterhouse steak while I ordered a chef salad. That did it. Ed started telling me how unhealthy he thought a vegetarian diet was. He lectured me on sleep, exercise, breaking bad habits, and, finally, how to discover if I was prone to the nineties addiction of codependency.

The tables for two were smashed together, and I realized that Ed was not only talking loudly enough for everyone to hear, but he was watching the people on either side of him eat, licking his lips at one point. Our food arrived, and he continued talking while he ate, revealing to me how steak looks at various stages of being chewed and mixed with saliva.

I was weary and grossed out, and thankful when he excused himself to go to the men's room, giving me time to get together an excuse to go home after dinner and avoid a nightcap at a bar.

Ten minutes later, Ed was walking back to our table, and I watched him vanish.

I craned my head, and saw that three tables down, he'd sat down with a woman who was eating alone and had the same color hair as me. That's how much attention the guy had paid to me—he couldn't remember who I was, hadn't even taken a good enough look at me.

The strangest part was, the woman never asked who he was or why he was sitting there, or why he picked up his conversation from where he'd left off earlier—how, earlier in the day, he'd outfoxed a used-car dealer. She was nodding and smiling and flirting, and Ed was lapping it up—until it was time for him to eat. He looked down and saw that he didn't have a plate.

He stood up, and turned slowly in place, his big diamond stud flashing. His face was scrunched with worry.

I let him rotate twice, avoiding his eyes when his gaze passed over me. Leaving him stranded was my payback for all his carelessness and lecturing. After a few seconds, I figured I'd tortured him enough, so I raised my hand and caught his glance.

He walked to our table, sat down, picked up his fork and started eating and talking as if nothing had happened. When he'd polished off his steak, he pushed his plate away, gave a low belch, and said, "Say, why don't you and me get married?"

I couldn't help it: I just laughed in his face.

—Esther, 37, advertising account executive, Long Island, New York

× × × × × × × × × ×

Roger, my ex-boyfriend, called at work and offered to set me up on a date. Considering Roger had dumped me, I got his drift: This was some charity move—he was doing me a favor.

Then I thought there was more to this. When Roger had called last week, even before this, to ask me back, I told him to take a hike. So the offer to fix me up with a date was also a slap to me: I had heard that he was dating like there was no tomorrow, and he had probably heard that I wasn't dating much. So his point was that at twenty-eight I had let my chance for big-time love—with him, of course, pass me by. He was taking a superior position and throwing me a date.

Rather than decline and sound defensive or mad, I decided to act laid back and accept his offer.

Roger told me that my prospective blind date, Willy, was a great all-American guy, a little younger than me, and an athlete. That's all I found out, because I had to get off the phone.

Willy called, and we lined up a time. On the night of our date, as I was getting ready, he phoned and asked me if I could pick him up. He didn't offer an excuse, so I went ahead and drove over.

Willy was dressed in a big T-shirt, Hawaiian shorts, and high-top sneakers, with no socks. He was bouncing on the balls of his feet as he motioned me to come in, and chirped, "Hi!"

I asked him how old he was, and he said, "Nineteen! I'm a sophomore! Is that fresh?! You're really thirty? Wow! Want a brewski?"

I asked why he had wanted me to drive, and he said, "I don't have a car! Want a dog or something?"

I passed on the "dog" and okayed the "brewski." I took a swig, and I was staring at a poster of Elle Macpherson. She was in one of those skimpy swimsuits that was wet and pulled into an even skimpier fit. Her nipples were erect in the poster, and Willy's scholarly impulses had clearly come alive. Over each nipple Willy had scrawled one word. The poster read, "Study . . . hard."

Call me psychic, but I figured we'd be going Dutch treat that night, so I let him take the lead when he suggested a greasy spoon around the corner. We got in my car, and I said, "Fasten your seat belt," like I always told my nephew.

We sat in a booth, and Willy made me glad I'm a woman as soon as he started talking. He filled me in on the nuances and thrills of peewee football when he was a kid. Of a fingernail-crunching eighth-grade baseball game that he remembered as if it were yesterday. Then, in excruciating detail, he slowly brought me up to date on thrilling high school games, creeping through his college track-team triumphs.

I asked if the small Band-Aid on his chin was a sports injury.

"Cut myself shaving," he said. "I don't really have to shave, but sometimes I like to, anyway. My mother buys me shaving stuff for my birthday, so I have a ton of it lying around."

I wanted to strangle Roger.

Willie said, "So, an older woman like you could really help, you know. And Roger says you'd benefit, too. And the best part is, you'd be showing me the ropes and giving me the sexual experience I need so I can date girls my own age. That'd be really fresh!"

—Peggy, 30, doctor of family medicine, Salt Lake City, Utah

× × × × × × × × × ×

After I'd had two dates with her, her brother is the one who told me, "You ease out of it now, or you marry her, or you find a way for her to dump you. But don't ever be the one to break up with her later. And you didn't hear it from me."

What a pill. His sister was wonderful. Pretty, smart, though a little on the shy side.

But I was only twenty-three, and after eight months I wanted to date other people. I wasn't in a marrying mood. I explained this to her, and she said she understood, and of course we could still see each other while we dated other people.

Well, this would work out fine for me. Because if I didn't have other women around to date, I could still date her. I guess that's where my thinking broke down.

Around midnight the noise woke me up. I went to my window and at first couldn't make out what was happening.

She had parked beside my car, and was standing outside her car, opening and closing her door, banging her door into mine repeatedly. I just stood at the window, thinking that if I went out, we'd have a scene, and the situation would only get worse.

She got back in her car, and I went back to bed, deciding to deal with my car door tomorrow.

I waited to hear her car moving into the distance, but instead I heard a crash. I went to the window again.

I finally noticed that she wasn't in her car, she was in a four-wheel-drive Bronco.

She had turned around and was using the back end of the Bronco to crunch into the back end of my Korean subcompact. While I was hopping into a pair of pants, she pulled away, jumped the curb, and drove straight for the side of my car. She bashed it in, pushing it against a tree, then backed up and bashed it again. She did this one more time, then backed up, and fishtailed the back of her car into the front of mine.

Then she drove away.

The next day a mechanic came out and told me the car was totaled. The chassis and the motor were shot.

I took another look at the knotted mess that had been my car and reevaluated my last conversation with my girlfriend. Obviously breaking up with her had been a bad idea, and I couldn't think of a way to have made her dump me that wouldn't have incited her to do something like this.

Maybe I should have married her. Or maybe I should have been less of a jerk myself.

—Kurt, 33, rancher, Wyoming

× × × × × × × × × ×

Holly always packs the house with friends and relatives. That way the management thinks her band is hot. That's what she tells me.

She has been after me for nearly a year to come hear her play. She has also been trying to get a date with me for months, and I might go out with her sometime if she would just back off a little and stop sticking to me like gum on my shoe every time I run into her.

She's the roommate of one of my buddies, and their arrangement is strictly platonic. Sometimes she tags along with him if he's meeting me.

I've never been to hear her band, Holly and the Good Time Boys, play.

I hate the name of the band, and I just don't want to hear them. I have a thing about garage bands—if you've heard one, you've heard them all. Mostly, I make it a policy never to get in this rut where, having gone once, you're expected to go to every one of their performances for the rest of your life or you're self-centered. I don't make my friends come to my bank. Friends in garage bands—and I must know five aspiring rock stars—can be a pain and more trouble than they're worth.

She has a gig tonight and has been pressuring me big-time to make it. I say okay. Anything to chill her out.

She called this morning to double-check that I was coming and to tell me the schedule: Her band goes on at 8:00, she'll have a ticket for me at the door, and afterward we'll go get a bite together.

I try to prepare her for the chance that I might not show up by saying that I might be a few minutes late.

Holly says, "That's okay. I'll play till you get there. I want you to hear us."

That night I don't feel like going. I'm working late, and a friend asks if I want to get a drink with him. We go have some beers, then have dinner. At 9:30 I tell him about Holly and ask if he wants to stop by with me.

It's 9:45 when we get to the door of the club where Holly's playing. I'm doing my duty, after all. I'll stay a few minutes, then get out.

It's not the kind of show I expected. A few audience members are heckling her, and the microphones on Holly's band are so loud they're kind of painful. Holly has a mean look on her face. Tomorrow I'll have to tell her that her shows are more like hostile performance art that inspires audience participation.

I sidle over to a wall, and she catches my eye. I give her a little smile, and her face lights up for a second, then a black cloud comes over her face. Uh-oh.

There are more band members than there ought to be. And one of the bigger guys is trying to take the guitar away from one of the Good Time Boys.

The Good Time Boy says an obscenity that the mike picks up, Holly sings even louder, and the Good Time Boys start trading blows with those extra guys.

Some of the audience is on its feet, cheering the extra guys, and other people in the audience—Holly's friends and family, no doubt—are yelling at the hecklers to shut up. Fights are breaking out in the audience.

Hey, this is more fun than I thought it'd be. Think I'll get another beer and stick around.

Holly jumps off the stage and marches toward me. Is she going to ask me if I want her to autograph my shirt or something?

"You're late," she says, flared up. "You knew I'd play till you got here. The headliners are mad at me, and the management is furious, and I probably won't get to play here again because of you."

I say, "Well, sorry," and that's when red and silver stars blink against my eyeballs, and the lights go out.

My bed is a rock, and I hear my buddy say, "You got hit. We're in the parking lot."

Holly had KO'd me. I didn't even see the punch coming. My jaw is killing me.

My friend tells me that maybe I shouldn't stand up.

Sitting on that parking lot, letting what he just said sink in, my thinking becomes crystal clear. Three new rules for living come to my mind: One, never standup a date. Two, have respect for bands of every caliber. Three, don't forget that treating someone badly can boomerang and come back to get you in the jaw.

—Luke, 19, bank teller, Memphis, Tennessee

× × × × × × × × × ×

As I was moving into my apartment, the previous tenant was moving out. I was furious that he hadn't cleared out, but he seemed so frail and apologetic that I didn't call the super.

He stopped by a total of three times. Once to get a clay pot he'd left, once to see if there was any mail for him, and once to say he had left a key to his safe deposit box taped under a kitchen drawer and needed to get it.

He didn't annoy me much, because he seemed harmless and earnest, but he was irritating me just a little bit, and I hoped he would quit coming to my apartment.

The fourth time he stopped by, he tapped on a box he was holding and told me that he had picked up some things from the building supervisor, and had come by my apartment to ask me out on a date.

I didn't want to go out with him, and so I used the basic lie of having a boyfriend.

He nodded and said, "Fair enough. Just thought I'd ask. Mind if I use the bathroom for a second?"

I let him in, and he left the room. He returned immediately and said, "I think one of the pipes broke. There's water all over the bathroom floor. Come look."

I went in the bathroom. Out of the corner of my eye I saw him make a low movement, then the lights went out, and the door slammed. I felt for the light switch and turned it on, then yanked on the door handle, but he was holding it shut from the outside.

I heard an odd scuffling and let go of the door knob when I saw about ten little mice scurrying around the bathroom floor and running over my shoes.

I screamed and pulled myself onto a counter, lifting my legs straight out.

"I'll show myself out," he said from the other side of the door.

I sat on the counter with my heart beating, wondering how I could get out of the bathroom without having to put my feet on the floor, and how I could escape without letting the mice into the rest of my apartment.

I had a classic terror of mice, and he had anticipated getting a classic brush-off. Rather than show up with a box of candy, he'd shown with a gift more suitable to the occasion: a box of mice.

—Wanda, 39, insurance agent, Rhode Island

9

The fates conspire—with you, for once

A Happy Ending

You've overcome snowballing ordeals, appalling personalities, mortifying circumstances, unfortunate surprises. In fact, you've sworn off dating . . . but here you are, getting ready to go out on yet another date. What keeps you going is knowing that you're not alone, that everyone has suffered through a Date from Hell. You're willing to take the risk in the hope that this date, this time, is heaven-sent. Because you know your luck is bound to be red-hot sometimes. And sometimes it is.

Just another Saturday night with a buddy—that was how I usually spent my Saturday nights. It's not as if I never met women I wanted to go out with. I did. But it was difficult to meet women I liked and also wanted to wake up next to: nice could be boring; sexy could turn out to be vain or manipulative. It had been a year and a half since my last serious relationship.

I was picky. I didn't like bar scenes or parties too much, which further narrowed my opportunities. Besides, I was getting used to my solo life.

Of course, as any single person can tell you, your apartment can start to feel like a cage. So I had started to frequent this neighborhood Mexican restaurant and had gotten to know Lupe, the owner. She knew my favorite table by the window—and placed my usual order the moment I came in. Over a year, I'd been going there two or three times a week, alone or with friends.

One Saturday in February, as I flagged Lupe for more salsa and chips, I looked across the tiny restaurant, and there, two tables away, was the woman of my dreams. She was laughing, and I couldn't take my eyes off her. She had short, pixieish brunette hair, and big warm eyes, and she had an appealing quality that kept my attention glued to her. I was in love.

She caught my eye and looked startled. Then she looked back at me, casually studying me for a few seconds.

My friend told me to go introduce myself, but I wasn't about to; the woman was with a man. I didn't have enough guts to strong-arm her date and ask for her number.

Over the next half hour she and I engaged in heavy eye contact, to the point where her date turned and looked around the room, trying to figure out what she was staring at, and I scrutinized my burrito as if I'd never seen one before in my life.

On her way back from the restroom, I got to see that she was medium height, slim, and had a killer figure. I also got a surprise, because as she walked back to her table—so slowly I thought I was going to die—she was staring directly at me.

My friend and I left, and as I walked in front of the restaurant's window I glanced in and saw that she was looking at me. I kept walking, then turned around and stuck my head against the window and waved, and immediately thought to myself, *What a stupid thing to do.*

I had a beer with my friend and spent the next two hours obsessing. If only I'd been a pick-up kind of person who could have confidently ignored her date, held out a matchbook and asked her to write down her phone number on it. If only I'd made some real contact with her. If only I hadn't stuck my head in the window and waved like I was a geek.

After a sleepless night, the next morning I went to the restaurant and asked Lupe if she remembered the woman. Lupe said that Saturday nights were always crowded, and she wasn't sure if she knew which woman I was describing. I told Lupe that if she ever did see the woman again, to please ask her to leave her number with the restaurant. Lupe was skeptical, naturally. "Oh sure! The first miracle will be that I recognize her, the second that the woman just hands over her phone number for you."

She had a point.

I stepped up my pace, going to Lupe's restaurant every other night if I could, on the off-chance of seeing the woman again. I managed to make every meal last two hours. One week went by. Then two. Neither Lupe nor I ever saw the woman again. This was New York City, not some small town where our paths were guaranteed to cross again at some point.

Suddenly all my friends were telling me about a man or a woman they'd seen on a bus, on the subway, in a store or bank, and had been smitten with, and had never seen again. The message was for me to get over it and pull myself out of my torment.

But I couldn't get her out of my mind. I was at the restaurant so often, Lupe asked me if I wanted to get my mail delivered there. I filled a journal with my nightly musings about that woman. I was haunted. Normally, I consider myself to be a very practical guy, but I had this ridiculous fantasy that she was the one, that I would marry her—whoever the heck she was.

Twice, I thought I saw her. The first time, I jumped to my feet at the restaurant, pushed through the crowd at the door, and presented myself with a too boisterous "*Hi!*" to the wrong woman. I explained that I thought she was someone else, and when she told Lupe she wanted a table for one person, I felt so guilty about making a scene that I invited her to join me. I suffered through a dinner where my companion talked endlessly about her swamp studies in Cape Cod. When her back was turned, I actually ordered aspirin with our last round of drinks.

The second time, I thought I saw her going into the restaurant as I was going out, but it was a teenager.

At the end of four weeks, on a crummy, snowy Friday night, I took my seat by the window and opened my newspaper. I had faced the facts. I had let go of the prospect of my mystery woman, and had even arranged to hit a singles-type bar that weekend. Lupe raced to my table, and with an ear-to-ear grin, said, "My friend! I have good news. It happened."

She handed me her restaurant's business card, and on the back were a couple of sentences I couldn't decipher.

"It's in French," Lupe told me, giving me a beer on the house. "It says, 'I look forward to seeing you again. I love folk singers.—Marie.' "

Lupe looked excited, but my enthusiasm took a dip. On one hand, the idea of a French woman was romantic, on the other hand, what was this folk singer reference? I was in restaurant equipment sales.

Lupe shrugged and told me to bring Marie there on our first date.

I wasn't sure if there would be a first date. I supposed I could quickly learn one basic folk song if I tried, but I did not speak French. My stomach was in knots. What a mess.

To make matters even worse, what if it wasn't the right person? Now that I was about to come face-to-face with the woman of my dreams, I was getting cold feet.

I let two days go by. I didn't want to seem too eager, and

I wanted to stop being panicky. I told myself not to expect too much.

I called the office number, asked for Marie, and she did have an accent, but it wasn't French.

I said, "Hi. This is Tommy. You gave your number to Lupe so that I could call you. I'm that guy who had that eye contact thing with you." I smacked my palm against my forehead. What a stupid thing to say. What happened to the smooth opening I had rehearsed?

She said she remembered, but that she was pressed for time at work and couldn't talk, and suggested we meet for dinner at the restaurant the next night. There was a lot of background noise, and I could barely hear her. I still didn't have a clue what her personality was like.

When I arrived, she was already there. Lupe had seated her at my table by the window. She was in the chair I always dumped my coat on when I ate alone.

When I stumbled through a French greeting and asked if she were from Paris, she laughed and said she was from Austin, Texas. She'd written the note in French because she thought *I* was French; she'd seen me put on a beret—that's my winter hat—when I'd left the restaurant. And she thought she'd overheard me talking about my career as a folk singer.

With the language and singing barriers behind us, we had a great dinner. She confided that she'd known I'd been watching her that night when she walked back to her table, and that she'd been afraid of the same things I'd been wary about: that she'd never see me again, or that if she did I might be a nightmare. She was as interesting, sexy, and nice as I'd hoped, and I couldn't believe my luck. I had no idea what she thought of me—probably that I was an obsessive nut, a nice guy she'd have to give the brush-off.

I took her out for a drink that night, and as I put her in a cab afterward, she reached up and kissed me.

We went out twice a week for over a month before we spent the night together. But it was only a few days later that we said we loved each other, only six months until she moved into my apartment, and six more months before I proposed to her, and she accepted—at Lupe's restaurant, of course, at our table by the window.

—Tommy, 33, restaurant equipment sales, New York City